The Year of 500 Fish

The Year of 500 Fish

HOW I REKINDLED MY LOVE OF FISHING

NATHAN WOELFEL

Nathan Woelfel
Sheboygan Falls, WI

Contents

Acknowledgements

No one accomplishes anything worthwhile without the help of others. Putting together a book that I am truly passionate about has long been a goal of mine and I wouldn't have realized this dream without encouragement from some amazing people.

First, I want to thank my wife Lyza. No matter what my newest adventure is, you are always by my side cheering me on, lifting me up, and guiding me toward what I am truly chasing.

I'd like to thank Steve Hill, my mentor, editor, and friend. Your patience, wisdom, expertise and encouragement have helped me navigate the twists and turns of my writing career. Through your efforts, these stories came to life.

Finally, I'd like to thank my family for being a continual source of love and support. No matter what I am trying to tackle, you have always been there with endless love and enthusiasm. Achieving this goal means even more, knowing that I get to celebrate it with you.

Introduction

"How many fish do you think you've caught in your life?"

I posed this question to my dad one night while relaxing at my parents' house over a couple of after-dinner drinks.

The setting sun shined brightly through the living room window of their home on the west side of Sheboygan Falls, just minutes away from my house. The light reflected sharply off the wood floors as reruns of The Price is Right played on the TV.

The walls of the nearby stairway are filled with fish, deer, and duck mounts. Each one of them is a special trophy filled with joyous memories. They are all a product of my dad's application of the knowledge passed along to him by our family's elders. I was part of many of those stories. I am well-versed in the lands and waters that produced these notable harvests.

He took a sip of his brandy old-fashioned sweet before answering, the ice rattling in his glass.

"I don't know, maybe 1,000, probably a few more than that."

That answer seemed on the low end to me. Throughout his five-plus decades on this earth, my father had spent much of his free time in the pursuit of fish. He, in turn, shared that passion with me, and that's how my affinity for the outdoors took root.

Like him, I was born and raised in Wisconsin and have called Sheboygan County home for most of my life. We're just miles away from beautiful Lake Michigan and all its glorious fishing bounty. One of its larger tributaries, the Sheboygan River, has several accessible spots within a short walk or bike ride from my childhood home. The Sheboygan's muddy, coffee-colored waters are where I cut my teeth in the fishing game. As a kid, I created many memories of catching panfish near the rocky shoreline of the local lagoon and chasing smallmouth bass just below the dam in a nearby park.

I consider myself incredibly fortunate to have such an important figure in my life who continues to be so willing to share his enthusiasm and knowledge with me. In fact, the bond we built over hunting and fishing was the subject of one of the first magazine articles I ever got published.

As I continue to write more stories related to the outdoors, I look back and see that my dad is a central figure in many of them. While I was flying solo on many of the adventures detailed in this book, my dad is featured in pretty much every chapter that involves other people.

To me, fishing is intended to be a social endeavor. My entire immediate family participates in it at some level.

Before I could drive, my mom spent many a summer morning shuttling my friends and me to a fishing hole so we could enjoy a day outside of the house. I still recall many of those outings fondly and in great detail.

I remember one time, probably when I was 12 or 13 years old, that I somehow convinced my sister to join me on a trip to Esslingen Park on the Sheboygan River to pursue king salmon during the fall run. My sister, a little more than two years my junior, spent the afternoon casting spoons with me as the large fish jumped all around us. We didn't catch anything that day, but it's still a moment I remember and treasure because, while we have spent a lot of time on the water together with our family, I'm not sure my sister and I have shared a fishing trip, just the two of us, ever since.

Most of my friends partake in fishing, if only on occasion. Once we all had our driver's licenses, there was a good stretch of time when I would fish at least weekly with a group of buddies. We chased out to the piers on cold spring afternoons hoping to connect with one of Lake Michigan's several strains of rainbow trout. We'd carp-fish in the summer and target pike and bass in the fall on the shores of the Sheboygan while munching away on pork rinds or other gas station snacks. These trips were one of the first ways we asserted our newfound freedom as we transitioned toward adulthood.

Whether the action is hot or the fishing is slow, sharing experiences with the right people can make every trip more enjoyable.

For as long as I can remember, fishing has been a choice activity for me in my free time. I'm definitely not a pro; nor do I desire to be one. Though I'm confident that I am an above-average angler. Not because of my skill, necessarily, but because of the persistence that comes from my curiosity and the natural desire I have to invest time in fishing.

When fishing is on my mind, there's no stopping me from being near the water. I keep at least one fishing rod and a tackle box in the bed of my silver Ford F-150 throughout the duration of the open water season. This allows me the chance to slip away for a quick session during lunch breaks or small portions of available time that would have otherwise been spent on some other pursuit.

Summer nights without a fishing trip often feel like wasted evenings to me. I try to avoid that feeling as much as possible.

I'll be the first to admit there are plenty of people better at fishing than I am. Take my old college roommate JT, for example. He is a dedicated fisherman with knowledge of bass fishing that far exceeds my level of expertise.

Many humbling trips on Lake Michigan have ended with treks to the fish-cleaning station where fellow anglers greeted us by unloading full coolers of large fish that eluded us during our hours on the water. Each of these people has something that I don't, whether it is a piece of knowledge, a specific technique, or a better method of game-planning.

Realizations like these, coupled with the awareness that I need to shut up and listen to these folks while doing my best to learn from them, have accelerated my growth in the sport and have strengthened my commitment to fishing while helping me become more successful.

Though the exact time I invest on the water varies from year to year, I can't remember a single summer when fishing hasn't played a central role. Whether it was out on my grandpa's blue and white Wellcraft on the big lake, or puttering around on the shores of many of the local inland water sources that held a nice variety of fish, I have always needed to get my fix.

Like many people, I suddenly found myself with an abundance of time as winter turned to spring in 2020. The COVID-19 pandemic turned my regular schedule upside down. Many of the activities that provided mental respite were off the table. Normalcy, in any sense, was hard to come by at times. Even though I wouldn't be able to share as much of my time outside joined by family and friends, I made a conscious effort to put time into rekindling my fire for the outdoors. In the process, I had more rewarding experiences than I ever imagined possible. Through reading, testing new techniques, trying new spots, and experimenting with fresh lures, I increased my fishing knowledge and learned about myself in the process.

During this particular fishing season, I caught several personal-best fish, fished (and placed) in my first-ever bass tournament, and began my own outdoors brand. What follows is a glimpse into how all of these things came to be.

While I didn't set out with a specific number of fish that I wanted to catch in that season, the year culminated with me having a specific goal. The target evolved as the season pushed on. It added purpose while so many strange and unfortunate things were happening in the world. As the number grew, so did my sense of pride, along with my drive to increase my total. What started as a welcomed distraction from the day-to-day became a much-needed source of balance in my life.

My conversation with my dad had me hellbent on tracking each and every fish I caught. If anyone ever posed the same question to me that I posited to my dad, I wanted to be able to give a more definitive answer. In my eyes, I spend far too much time fishing to not know what, from a numeric standpoint, I was getting in return.

This book is about the 500-plus fish I caught during 2020, but don't worry. This won't be a play-by-play of each and every fish. Frankly, that's not that interesting. I will try to stick to the highlights as well as the memorable and teachable moments. It's important to me that I get to share all of this with you.

While some of the stories that follow depict fish that I did not personally catch—rather, ones caught in my company—I want to note that those fish did not count toward my total. (I have a separate tally for that. I'm a numbers person, so I'm a bit geeky that way.)

I will be the first to gloat that 500 fish in a year is not a milestone to turn your nose up at. But I want to be clear that

I went on plenty of fruitless ventures throughout this fishing season. No matter how long we fish, push our limits and expand our horizons, sometimes we just come up empty. Still, every trip finds a way to become a story or a lesson learned. Some are just better and more notable than others. Here I present what I consider the most compelling adventures that came from my added time in the outdoors.

My hope is that, whether you fancy yourself a hardcore angler or have never picked up a fishing rod in your life, you will find this book to be a unique mix of relatable fish stories, fishing tips, and maybe even a little life advice.

Some of these stories were written right after they happened; others came together a bit later, after I had time to reflect upon my experiences or look back on the notes in my fishing journal (which is something I highly encourage everyone to have, by the way).

I am passionate about sharing my love for the outdoors with others and words, both written and spoken, are how I choose to do that. As I relive these special moments, I want you to join me in the thick of the action.

This particular year of fishing changed my life forever. With each passing year, I find myself fishing more than I ever have, spending hundreds of hours on the water and loving every second of it. I have had the good fortune of sharing my affection for fishing with countless others and it has brought me immeasurable joy.

Perhaps these stories will trigger memories and thoughts of your favorite places and help you experience the warm feelings that come with positive recollections. Better yet, maybe this will help you discover or reignite your passion for fishing.

But before we hit the water, let's take a closer look at the journal that established the foundation for these stories.

CHAPTER 1

The Journal

Before we get into the stories (and there are plenty of them), It's important to get into their origins.

These tales are all highlights of the 500-plus fish I caught during the pandemic-stricken year of 2020. Some of the stories were written as soon as they happened. Many of them came together long after the fact, largely due to entries in my fishing journal.

Notes captured in my journal spark both memories and new insights. All these are the basis for the stories that follow.

Journaling is a great way to self-reflect on any aspect of life. It's a method of taking stock of where you've been, how you got there, and where you're going. It can assist in getting thoughts in order while providing tangible proof of progress and growth.

Throughout the years, I have come across articles in many publications regarding the importance of keeping an outdoors log, though I will admit this is the first time I have managed to keep one throughout an entire season.

Sure – not everyone writes a book. But a fishing journal is a great way to preserve the surprising amount of information that can come from every fishing adventure. Just as importantly, it's a proven method of capturing memories.

As I have become more dedicated to recording my results and observations, my journal has become something of a bible for me. It is the source of truth and official record of not only what happened but, what worked and what didn't.

While missing out on a few details may not make or break an angler when swapping fish stories with your buddies at a bar (some would argue those stories are sometimes even better that way), the specifics are crucial to finding repeatable fishing success when out on the water.

As of this writing, I've been trying to keep an outdoors log for the better part of the last four hunting and fishing seasons.

Through years of trial and error, I've discovered a few tips that helped me stick with it. I'm hoping these might help you as well.

Recognize the importance

Keeping an outdoors log is a great way to preserve recollections of time outside. But it also provides a chance to step back, scan the big picture and make decisions accordingly.

When the fishing is consistently slow, a journal can be a great place to turn for inspiration or potential solutions. A quick look back at a log will be a wonderful refresher course on recent activity

Maybe you are fishing the same spot a little too often. If you've been hitting up the same body of water with nothing but drowned worms or freshly washed lures to show for it, it might be time to move on.

It's possible a change in tactics might be in order.

Perhaps a certain bait works well in the morning, but doesn't seem to produce in the afternoon. The location on the pierhead while the waves gently lap against the pier is more of a sunrise spot, while the spot amongst the brush on the big bend of the river is better just before dusk. The last time a front came through, the action was best before the rain, not after it.

It could be time to come to grips with the fact that your favorite bait just isn't producing. Capturing the proper details in a journal allows you to quickly see how often you're leaning on a certain lure or presentation.

You'll be surprised at the trends that come flying off the page when revisiting your journal. These can help set you up for future success.

Make it easy

The simpler it is to access your log, the more likely you are to continue using it.

Pick a medium that works for you. It could be hand-written entries in a notebook or a full-blown spreadsheet.

I keep my journal in a Google Sheet. This spreadsheet resides in a digital cloud, which allows me to access it, wherever I go, by phone or laptop. This is especially useful when I need to record or review information quickly.

For several years, when we went out on Lake Michigan, my dad used to record each of our catches on a medium-sized notepad. Wanting to capture all of the details, he often attempted to jot down notes while we were out on the water. Sometimes, he would even dictate to me or my mom as we played the role of scribe. But the constant bumping and shifting of the waves can make handwriting illegible. The digital format solves for this by taking penmanship out of the equation. Entries can even be logged by transcribing voice recordings.

My Google Sheet allows me to link to corresponding photos on my Google Drive for a visual reminder of each trip.

If you're the type who pines for the romantic notion of putting pen to paper by candlelight while enjoying a nice cigar and sipping smooth bourbon, there are plenty of fancy leather-bound notebooks made for this specific purpose.

As for me, I will stick with my technology. I prefer having my clean and legible information available to me at a moment's notice wherever I go.

Start early

I'll admit that this year's robust journal did not start with the first fishing excursion of the season. I was so excited to be back on the water that I fell back into my old habits of looking forward to the next trip instead of reflecting on the last one.

This can impact the reliability of observations that ultimately get recorded. Typically speaking, the sooner thoughts are jotted down, the clearer and more accurate they are. Days after the fact, it's difficult to recall the finer points of a fishing trip, particularly when the action is good. Did half of my fish come on the pink jig or was it the orange one I switched to after I had to re-tie following a snag? The answers to these questions are always easier to pull out of the memory bank in the immediate aftermath.

However, the journal began to come together after my second trip.

Beginning to record as early in the season as possible not only helps ensure accuracy and the ideal level of detail for entries, it also begins to form the habits necessary to keep up with your log throughout the season.

Getting too far down the road without forming these habits makes catching up tough, if not impossible.

Be consistent

While any data or observations can be useful (we'll get to that in a moment), consistency is key.

Before you begin logging, identify the types of information

that are most important to you. Then do your best to record that information after every adventure.

For instance, my fishing log entries consist of the date, time I was fishing, body of water, target species, number of fish caught, baits I was using, weather conditions, and a section for relevant notes and observations that may be helpful in the future.

This will make comparisons easier and will help trends become more apparent.

Get detailed

The more detailed you can get with entries, the better.

Don't assume your future self will remember a key piece of information. If you're anything like me, that tidbit will probably get lost in the shuffle after a few more trips, then disappear forever. Jot it down while it's fresh and save yourself the trouble.

Details bring the story to life and can help spark additional memories that may be useful or simply enjoyable.

For example, on one trip to the Sheboygan River, I saw a bald eagle perched in the dead tree across the bank when I arrived. This was an unusual sight, so I noted it in my log. I spent time marveling at the sheer size of the bird instead of making sure my setup was on point. But it was a welcomed distraction.

This little note, while not relevant to fishing directly, helps bring forth a more vivid recollection of the location, weather, time of day, and other details.

But not too detailed

While details are crucial, don't let the pursuit of perfection get in the way of you completing a journal entry.

Any information you can provide your future self could prove valuable, even if it's not complete.

Yet this is a balancing act. The more granular you get, the

harder it can become to skim notes in a time-effective manner. Sometimes you need quick answers and don't have the time or need to sort through every last detail of the previous outing.

This balance will become easier to achieve through dedicated practice.

The important thing is to not be discouraged and work with what you have. You'll thank yourself later.

Now that you have an understanding of how the origins of these tales were documented, what do you say? Let's go fishing.

CHAPTER 2

Ice Fishing

Fish Nos. 1-2

Those who know me are well aware that ice fishing isn't exactly my favorite activity. Call me Captain Obvious but ice fishing, by its very nature, is often cold. And when it's cold, everything about fishing becomes more difficult. Wet lines freeze almost instantly. Ice builds up on the eyelets of the rods, making the simple act of moving a bait up or down a challenge. Wearing gloves may keep your hands warm, but you lose most of your dexterity. So you can forget baiting a hook or tying a knot. Toughing it out minus the gloves may be helpful for a short while, but you'll pay for it when you can't feel your fingers.

These are just a few of the reasons you won't hear me discussing ice fishing often. My bad attitude toward the hard water is often the butt of my fishing buddies' jokes. While I probably haven't given it a fair shake, I haven't enjoyed nearly the success on the ice that I have in the warmer months.

Given all of this, it's ironic that such a special year of fishing began with an ice fishing trip.

For me, ice fishing is more of a social activity – a great way to spend time with friends outside in the winter months and a convenient excuse to drink beer during the daytime on Saturdays.

Most of my ice fishing experiences consist of camping out on the ice with a group of my friends during the morning, drinking assorted light beer (or mimosas, if we're feeling classy), and grilling encased meats while we wait for the orange flags to pop on our tip-ups.

Our sausage of choice is, of course, bratwurst. My friends and I grew up in the shadows of Sheboygan, "the Bratwurst capital of the world." Brats are a staple of our community's culture. They are commonplace at family picnics, fundraisers, and sporting events. If you go to a local gathering in Sheboygan County that features food, I'll bet you all of the money in my wallet you will find a brat.

Bratwursts are a part of our culture here. Many organizations host brat fries as fundraisers. In fact, the annual Sheboygan Falls Fire Department Brat Fry is the social event of the year in my town of just over 7,000 people.

Each year, during the first week of August, this german sausage gets its own weekend-long celebration: "Brat Days." There's live music, carnival games, plenty of beer, and even a parade.

In our area, there are two primary players in the bratwurst market: Miesfeld's and Johnsonville. Miesfeld's has been making their sausages in Sheboygan since 1941. Shopping at their local meat market is like taking a step back in time. There's a full-service deli counter accompanied by a lengthy case of fresh-cut meat and friendly staff that is ready to answer all of your questions to make sure you leave satisfied with your purchases.

My dad and I take our venison trim to Miesfeld's annually. Over the years, Meisfeld's experts have transformed our deer into all sorts of delectable products, including snack sticks, ring bologna, polish sausage, and, yes, venison bratwurst.

Johnsville is the other major name in the bratwurst world in this part of the country and, as the brand has taken on a larger national presence, is probably the one most are familiar with.

Since 1945, Johnsonville has been making sausage on the far west side of my hometown of Sheboygan Falls. I even worked on the line there briefly when I was between jobs as I transitioned from sports writing to marketing.

Seemingly everyone in my circle has their preferences between Miesfeld's and Johnsonville brats, but regardless of which camp my friends fall into, bratwursts are almost always the sausage of choice for social gatherings, including ice fishing.

Of course, brats are always better with beer. In the dead of winter, there's never an issue with beverages remaining cold. When the temperature really drops, we've resorted to placing the beer cans on or near the grill until they are thawed enough to be drinkable.

Now that I have demonstrated my passion for cuisine, it should come as no surprise that, on the ice, I view myself as more of the group chef and source of comedic relief than a fishing asset. The way I see it, my responsibility is to get the grill fired up before everyone gets hungry and make sure that everything is prepared properly. I take pride in this. After outdoor recreation, cooking and baking are two of my biggest passions.

I keep my head in the game when I'm tending the grill. Sure, I'll go out of my way to make wisecracks when the opportunity presents itself. But, when we are ice fishing with tip-ups, I am always scanning my surroundings.

Tip-ups come in a couple of different designs, but they all work the same way. There is a spool of line attached to a plastic or wood body. When the line is in the water, the spool stands straight up. On top of the body is a small flagpole that gets tucked underneath the top of the spool. When a fish strikes and the spool begins to move, the tension on the flagpole is released and the flag stands straight up.

Our rule is: the first one to the line gets to fight the fish and when there's a fish on the line, all bets are off. If you want in on the action, you need to drop what you're doing and run as soon as you see a flag up.

If a tip-up goes, I will be one of the first to give chase. On more than one occasion, the rubber soles of my boots simply couldn't handle the slick ice. In the midst of my pursuit, I'd lose all traction and go tumbling down to the cold, smooth surface, much to the amusement of my fishing partners.

Due to my general lack of enthusiasm surrounding this winter activity, I own almost no ice fishing equipment, save for a couple of tip-ups and a minnow bucket.

For all of its pain points, ice fishing does have a redeeming quality: the accessibility it provides levels the playing field for anglers of all types.

Don't have a boat? No problem. Once the ice is solid, essentially any lake can be accessed by simply walking right on. This adds many opportunities to fish spots that are off-limits during the open-water season.

I'm a firm believer that fishing can be for everyone who wants to give it a chance. Ice fishing helps make that possible and gives many people a way to enjoy the outdoors when perhaps they otherwise wouldn't. That is undoubtedly a positive thing.

During this season, I was offered a chance that intrigued me. My dad presented me with the opportunity to take a guided trip in Sturgeon Bay with Scott, his former voice coach from UW-Green Bay. I had never met Scott, but he came up in conversation on occasion when I was growing up. My dad loves telling the story about how, back in college, he would sometimes show up for his voice lesson only for him and Scott to decide they were going to go goose hunting instead.

This adventure would be outfitted by Captain Bret Alexander of Ice Fish Green Bay, a guide Scott had worked with in the past. I'm always a bit skeptical about any prospective ice fishing ventures. But it's hard to resist the calling when the guide's Facebook page is stacked with pictures of piles upon piles of fish.

Plus, I felt it unconscionable to turn down the chance to meet someone who played such a crucial role in my dad's development as a professional and a human being. This struck me as a unique opportunity and, if nothing else, for this reason alone I wanted in.

Green Bay is a tremendous and arguably world-class, fishery that I had never spent any time on. Monster walleye, muskies, and smallmouth bass worthy of a place on your wall all call these waters home. People come from around the country to fish Green Bay.

On this trip, whitefish were the primary target. I had never caught a whitefish, but I knew them to be excellent table fare, particularly when smoked.

Many of my discussions about ice-fishing Green Bay centered around trophy walleye. In an earlier time, yellow perch were also often the target of ice anglers on the bay. While big walleyes are still a major draw these days, the perch population has dwindled in recent decades. That's where whitefish entered the scene. These nomadic, opportunistic feeders can provide some seriously fast-paced action if you are in the right place at the right time, making them desirable for anglers of all experience levels.

These days, there are many guides who run several trips a day during the winter exclusively for whitefish.

All of this intrigued me. So I decided it was worth committing my time and money.

After driving about an hour and a half north from Sheboygan, my dad and I arrived at the meeting point well in advance of sun-up. We parked on the edge of a snowy side road. I had no clue where we were exactly but I assumed there was water somewhere nearby.

The group consisted of my dad, Scott, his friend Peter, and myself. My dad and I vacated the warm sanctuary of our heated SUV and strolled down the icy walkway toward the pickup truck parked directly in front of us. Once there, we exchanged greetings with the other pair that comprised our party. I couldn't distinguish faces amid the pre-dawn darkness, but that didn't stop us from trading pleasantries while we waited for our guide's team to arrive.

The wind was absolutely howling, producing a significant amount of white noise as it kicked up the loose, fluffy snow lying on top of the ice. If you turned the wrong direction, you would get a faceful of it.

The guide's crew picked us up in a slick UTV with treads to navigate the snow-covered ice. This rig was equipped with an enclosed cab, heaters, and windshield wipers, and it seated five if those in back were comfortable with making new friends. The driver shuttled us to a shack in a shallow portion of the bay to let us pursue walleye before the whitefish bite began in earnest.

The perks of ice fishing with a guide service quickly become apparent on any trip, but even more so when the weather is less than ideal. First and foremost, guides do virtually all of the work for you. They've scouted the location, have an intimate knowledge of where the fish are, and place multiple shacks accordingly. Then there's the equipment. Fish finders, rods, bait — it's all there waiting for you. You don't even have to drill your own holes. Lose a lure? No problem. Several pre-rigged rods await you. Just pick up another one and you're back in action. And none of this speaks to the experience and knowledge provided by guides who are worth their salt. This includes coaching on the proper techniques, gear, fish habits, and more. But the real pièce de résistance is the heated shacks. No matter how cold it gets outside, more often than not, you can fish in a t-shirt or light long sleeve. It's clean living.

As we settled into our shack, it felt like we were in a small cabin with its interior wood paneling and small windows on two sides. It was comfortable, but we found the walleye to be uncooperative. As my dad and Scott caught up, I joined the conversation when I felt it appropriate, chewing on some homemade beef jerky between interjections and additions to the discussion. I didn't want to interfere with an important reconnection. The pair discussed music, shared information on the whereabouts of their mutual connections, and swapped stories about their time in the outdoors. It was easy to see how the relationship between my dad and Scott had transitioned from mentor and student to a true friendship.

After a little more than an hour, we were back in the UTV and off to deeper waters to get in on the whitefish bite.

A short time later, we arrived at our new home and got situated. We were positioned above some 80 feet of water, much deeper than I imagined it would be. The clear ice yielded an amazing view of the first six feet or so of water below. In a way, it's an eerie feeling, catching merely a glimpse of the dark abyss that exists below your feet. Once in a while, a loud crack would come from the top of the frosty ice. It's just a sign that Mother Nature is placing more ice beneath your boots, even though it's unsettling. But, as one of my good friends likes to say, once the water is above your head, it's all the same.

In a weird way, I often find solace in that statement. I'm not going to spend my entire life fishing in less than six feet of water. Knowing that, in reality, there is little difference in fishing 7 or 700 feet of water, I am able to compartmentalize the potential risks and get on with fishing.

Armed with standard ice fishing spinning setups with a minnow-shaped lure tipped with wax worms, we went to work. Looking at our fish finders, it was apparent there were plenty of fish around. It was just a matter of when they became active. Eventually, they did.

The preferred technique for working our baits, we were told, was a series of pops. This meant aggressively ripping the bait upward with successive pulls. We were told to exaggerate this motion early in the day because, as we became fatigued throughout the trip, we were less likely to be presenting the lure in the proper fashion if we didn't start out a little over the top. As the bait drastically ripped up the water column, it would draw attention to itself. When the bait fluttered back to its starting position, many fish would feel emboldened to strike. If our locators showed evidence of a fish pursuing the bait, we were to continue moving the lure steadily upward, trying to entice the fish to bite before it got too far out of its comfort zone. There is a finite amount of energy a wild animal can responsibly expend in the pursuit of a meal.

Scott was the first one hooked up. Even though they aren't the largest species in the system, whitefish fight hard and when you're pulling them up from the depths, you're in for an enjoyable battle.

The silver bounty eventually made its way from the depths into our shack and was placed in our fish bucket.

Next, it was my turn. The bite was surprisingly subtle, but a bite nonetheless. I set the hook and enjoyed the fight. It's akin to going toe-to-toe with a bass, but without the added leverage of a full-size spinning rod. The fish didn't take drag, but it didn't roll over and accept its fate either. A few moments later, I pulled it through the hole. My first whitefish.

Though the fish was a mere 16 inches long, this was definitely a special moment. At the ripe old age of 28, many seasoned outdoorsmen don't get to experience many firsts. I was appreciative of this one. Getting to share that moment with my dad made it all the more meaningful.

As the day wore on, the wind continued to whip. The action was enough to keep us interested, but far from hot.

All told, we ended up with six fish, with a few misses to add to our tally. I was fortunate enough to score two of the fish. Scott generously supplemented our pair with a couple of his own he was willing to part with. These fish quickly made their way to the smoker at my in-laws' restaurant and were consumed. They lasted a matter of days. The naturally high oil content of whitefish makes them an ideal candidate for the smoker. The comforting aroma and flavor of the smoke adhere to that oil and provide a delicious result that is perfect on crackers, in omelets, or enjoyed as-is.

At this juncture, I hadn't even begun counting fish or keeping a journal. But, even though I didn't know it at the time, this was the start of the most special fishing season of my life.

It was a wonderful day. Sure, the fish count wasn't quite what we wanted it to be. But the time invested in getting to know

Scott, who is special to my dad and an excellent outdoorsman in his own right, was an experience I will treasure for the rest of my life. Between their catch-up chats, we swapped fishing and hunting stories and spoke about the world around us.

Scott shared his experiences hunting for whitetail deer in Saskatchewan that feature all-day sits in the treestand with little to no communication with the outside world available. He pulled out his phone and showed us a picture of a large buck he had taken on one of his most recent adventures.

My dad provided some highlights about our open-water fishing season on Lake Michigan, a frequent topic of conversation when we are catching up with outdoors-minded folks we haven't seen in a while.

I offered up some tales from the duck blind during the previous year, including my hunting group's annual trip to Castle Rock Lake in Central Wisconsin when we endured near zero-degree temperatures while stacking up a pile of nearly two dozen mallards.

We formed a bond that day over our common experiences and, to me, that is what the outdoors are all about.

Both my dad and I have fished with Scott several times since our first outing on Green Bay.

I am proud to say that, these days, I now consider Scott to also be a friend of mine. We exchange messages on social media about our hunting experiences and fishing trips we would like to take.

As I grow older, I've come to learn that in order to enjoy the outdoors to its fullest, they must be shared with others. I feel fortunate to have been introduced to Scott and to be able to add him to the circle of people who help deepen my love for hunting and fishing.

CHAPTER 3

Opening Day

Fish Nos. 3-4

There's just something about the anticipation of the first day of the inland fishing season. I view the day's annual arrival as something of a holiday that ushers in the true beginning of summer. The prospect of catching fish is just as exciting as the promise of warmer, longer days. It brings me energy.

The Opening Day of inland fishing in Wisconsin is the first Saturday in May. During this particular year, the official kickoff of my open water season came nice and early, on May 2.

There's a problem with relatively early openers, though. While many anglers are ready, the fish are not. It can be tough sledding in the month of May, even as the weather grows warmer and the sun appears for longer stretches of time.

High water levels can keep water temperatures low enough for fish to be sluggish or even flat-out dormant until late May or early June. It wasn't warm in the lead-up to the opener, so I wasn't terribly optimistic about my prospects. But I knew I was going to spend the bulk of the day giving it a try. After all, it had been nearly three months since I had been fishing. For whatever reason, I just hadn't prioritized making the time to get outside and wet a line. In the coming weeks, that quickly changed.

I had two separate plans of attack. The first was to fish for pike. I was hoping to find a few that had recently spawned and perhaps were a little more willing to strap the feedbag on, even in colder temperatures. By casting and retrieving, I could cover more water and increase my chances of encountering a hungry fish.

My second idea was to utilize nightcrawlers. It's a scouting strategy I often use when trying to gain my bearings since so many species will gladly chomp on a worm if given the opportunity. The way I see it, if you can't get a bite on a worm, there probably aren't many active fish around.

This method also allows for otherwise sluggish fish to approach the stationary bait on their own terms. The lack of movement also gives the nightcrawler a chance to disperse its scent into the surrounding water, hopefully producing a strike.

With that in mind, I headed down to River Park—a place that, looking back on it, was a staple of my childhood. As a kid, I spent countless days here, running around the playground, hitting tennis balls with my Aunt Debby and, of course, fishing.

The Sheboygan River provides one of the borders of the property, necessitating a trio of bridges that allow access to the park. At one point, the river cuts underneath a small, white footbridge and forms a lagoon that generally holds a good number of small panfish.

For all intents and purposes, this is where I learned to fish. Some of my earliest fishing memories come from the time I spent with my parents or grandparents bobber fishing for bluegills or dangling little hooks tipped with kernels of corn between the rocks that line the lagoon.

With plenty of options and an entire season in front of me, I decided to work a stretch of the river that had been a pike and bass hotspot for me years before. The spot sits adjacent to one of Bemis Manufacturing's several plants in the city. An old shelter house overlooks the river bend that gives way to a straight stretch of water leading to a suspended pedestrian bridge that I refer to as "the swinging bridge." The far shoreline features a few yards of tall grass that transitions to more of a wooded setting. The park side of the shore is mostly grass dotted with a few weeping willows that are the bank's only defense against erosion during seasonal floods. Over the years, as the willows have come down, the evidence of their worth has become more obvious.

Back in middle school, before we knew any better, my friends and I would cast Pro King trolling spoons here and spend many hours catching "hammer handle" pike and even the occasional smallmouth. The lures were far too light for casting. Not the ideal bait choice, but we worked with what we had, and it proved to be effective.

But I have learned a lot since since then and, on this day, I spent nearly three hours traveling the shoreline, working around the occasional green picnic table or garbage can, tossing my best pike lures. I stuck with two of the classics: an orange and silver Little Cleo and the red and white Dardevle, while putting a dead rod with a nightcrawler on the bottom. I inched my way toward the bridge, occasionally adjusting the location of the dead rod when I felt it got out of range. None of this brought me any luck. Disappointing, but not overly surprising.

As I worked my way down the bank, my attention was drawn

to a series of noises across the river. After briefly searching for the source of the snapping twigs and rustling leaves, I spotted a family of deer that had wandered through an industrial area and into the safety of a small wooded plot on the far shore. They slowly meandered about, stopping on occasion to nibble on some food. From my vantage point, it was hard to identify their snack of choice, but it became clear that whatever was hiding underneath last year's dead leaves was of some value to them. Seeing deer in Wisconsin isn't hard, but this is the first time I can recall ever seeing them this close to the park.

That little interaction made its way into the notes section of my fishing journal. Yes, it was partly because of the slow fishing. But a part of me wanted to record one of the most memorable and special moments of my first trip of the open water season. It was so unexpected but it immediately brought back memories of sitting in my tree stand during the previous deer season. There's just something exciting about encountering another living thing and getting to observe its habits while your presence goes undetected. In this way, I was almost grateful for the lack of fish. It gave me time to look around and enjoy the world around me. Frankly, if you can't find some highlights and satisfaction from the slower days, you won't get much fulfillment from fishing.

But it's funny how those types of details seem to be harder to come by in my journal entries, as the season goes on. It's not that I don't appreciate all of the experiences that nature gives me; I just become a little less focused on the big picture. Looking back on my notes, it's kind of startling how quickly it becomes about the fish rather than the fishing. It's definitely something I want to avoid in future seasons.

With my morning trip completed, I returned home briefly to handle some yard work. I recently received a new rain gauge for my birthday and wanted to get it mounted to the wood fence that separates our yard from the back alley so that I could begin my daily precipitation recordings. With that project completed, I turned my attention to filling the bird feeder that hangs on one of the old metal laundry poles in the back.

After that, my wife joined me on a quick trip to visit the neighbors who live two doors down so that I could pay my entry fee into his yearly turkey hunting pool. It awards the sum of the money collected to the hunter who harvested the largest gobbler that season.

We found the pair sitting on their front porch each enjoying a Natural Light Strawberry Lemonade. After a short chat, I ventured out to the local bait shop, Terry's Bait & Tackle, and acquired some large fathead minnows, along with a few cold ones to sip while the fish weren't biting.

Terry's establishment is located a few miles west of Sheboygan Falls in Plymouth. The old shop, was situated near an old barn, down a short gravel driveway that can be accessed by either of the neighboring county roads. About a decade earlier, when I began spending time and money there, the storefront was little more than a shack. A wood-burning stove heated the joint, the near wall was filled with assorted basic fishing equipment, hooks, sinkers, bobbers, and the like.

Right after hunting season, it was not uncommon for the first few feet of the wall to be blocked by piles of raccoons harvested by local hunters and trappers. For added income, Terry would skin the animals and sell the pelts for what they were worth which, honestly, probably wasn't much.

Upon entering the building, I'm accustomed to receiving Terry's enthusiastic greeting of, "morning!" Even in the afternoon.

Next to the counter was an old recliner where Terry lounged

during his free time watching the TV fed by a satellite dish on the roof. In back, a homemade irrigation system kept the blue and black tanks of minnows supplied with a constant stream of fresh, aerated water.

The place has a laid-back atmosphere. I will never forget one of my first trips to Terry's. It was prior to sunrise on a winter morning and a group of friends and I made a quick stop to pick up some minnows on our way to the Glenbeulah Millpond. The neon sign said the store was open, but no one was inside. A bit confused, we headed back to the truck.

Just then, the door to the porta potty next to the entrance swung open, startling all of us. "Come on in! I'll be right there," bellowed Terry. Shortly after that, we had our bucket of minnows and were on our merry way.

All joking aside, Terry is more than willing to share the latest chatter on how the bite has been on a local lake or offer advice or assistance if you ask. But I always appreciate his willingness to let you browse the store and come to your own conclusions if you're in a bull-headed mood. You can be in and out in a matter of seconds or spend some time shooting the breeze. I like that.

As Terry's business has grown, so has his shop. A few years ago, the footprint of the business expanded. The building felt less like a repurposed shed and more like a proper retail space. The original store now sat just to the left of the new main entrance. That turned into a side room that still housed the recliner as well as the TV. The new addition featured small aisles that line the path between the door and the new location of the minnow tanks.

Eventually, Terry moved to a new location a few country blocks east of his old abode. His operation has really taken shape.

Though the footprint of the business has changed, Terry's still has the same hole-in-the-wall feel it has always had. It's the kind of place where I can feel confident I can find the supplies I need while talking fishing with anyone and everyone in the shop.

After making my way to the back of the updated space, I secured my minnows in a small red and white Coleman cooler I had laying around the garage.

The sun continued to shine and the conditions became increasingly beautiful, with temperatures now in the low 70s.

I was off to my in-laws' house. They live just down the road from us and have a gorgeous property nestled right on the shores of the Sheboygan. Since the day I began dating their daughter, I was always drawn to the river whenever I was at my in-laws' house. I just couldn't help but appreciate the beauty and the fishing potential of the property. Early on, it was made clear I was more than welcome to come fish there whenever I'd like. I married wisely, I know. In all seriousness, my in-laws are very hospitable people who have treated me accordingly from the jump. In addition to the wonderful home-cooked meals, free drinks, and family time, allowing me to come and go as I please for fishing purposes is just a small extension of how they have always treated me well since I became part of their family over a decade ago.

When I arrived at the river, I found the current was closer to fast than slow, typical of early May. It was slightly too fast to drift the minnow under a slip bobber, and definitely too quick to have hope of keeping a bottom rig in place. So I decided to concentrate my efforts on the few portions of slack water within reach, utilizing a single hook with a pair of sinkers to keep my fathead just off the bottom.

I slowly inched down what was left of the old wooden staircase just off the back patio and to the river bank. A few springs ago, as the floodwaters rose, the bottom third of the stairs was ripped clean off. There was a pool of slow water to the left of what is now the bottom step. That little spot had produced many a smallmouth for me over the years and I figured it to be my best chance at getting on the board.

As luck would have it, I was right. A quick flash appeared near the general direction of my minnow and the line got tight. At best, it was a modest fish, a smallie of about eight-to-nine inches in length. But it was my first fish of the open water season and it put a big smile on my face.

Later in the evening, nearly a dozen kayakers floated past, out enjoying the day. One pair was a father who was out with his young son pursuing some bass. Those kinds of scenes always warm my heart and take me back to when I was first starting out.

Suddenly, in my mind, I was right back at the lagoon with my dad gently guiding me through the basics of catching panfish with a simple hook and bobber setup. He would occasionally give me pointers while giving me space to do my own thing and learn by experience.

It's so comforting to see fishing traditions continuing to be passed on to future generations.

After a few more minutes without action, I decided to move down the river toward where the county road crosses the water. The bridge supports provided plenty of slack water. I lost a couple of bass, but was able to land one more before the sunset. It was similar in size to the one I caught earlier in the evening.

It felt good to feel the rush of seeing a rod tip bounce and the unique tension of a fish on the end of the line again. Though it was a slow start, the meat of my fishing season was underway.

CHAPTER 4

A Special Evening on Lake Michigan

Fish Nos. 14-15

Living just a handful of miles from the shores of one of the Great Lakes is a tremendous blessing. Having been in this area most of my life, it's easy to forget what a spectacle Lake Michigan truly is with its smooth, sandy beaches, the chilled water that often showcases itself in several hues of blue, and the peaceful white noise produced by the steady cadence of waves. All of it is just a short drive away.

I try my best not to take this good fortune for granted by spending as much time on or near the lake as possible.

While I devote a few hours each year on the beach relaxing or taking strolls on the boardwalk with my wife, most of my interaction with Lake Michigan comes through fishing with my family. Sure, there were plenty of summertime trips to the beach during my childhood, but my relationship with this special body of water has significantly strengthened through the time I have spent pursuing the salmon and trout it holds.

When considering our Lake Michigan fishing aptitude, I would say the Woelfels are slightly above average. We've gained a lot of knowledge through our years on the lake and we nearly always head out on the water with a solid game plan that includes an idea of what baits to run, which water temperatures we are looking for, and the speeds at which the boat should be moving while trolling.

We generally return home with at least a couple of fish in the cooler. Getting skunked is rare, but so is limiting out. We know what we're doing, but I would never dream of calling us experts.

For most of my life, we exclusively fished Lake Michigan out of the port of Sheboygan.

The facility is quite well kept, with two spacious parking lots featuring extra-long stalls to house trucks and trailers, a fish cleaning station with bathrooms and running water, and several different docks to tie up your boat before or after launching.

Dozens of boats dot the water just off the launches as they enjoy their seasonal slips in the marina. These spaces are occupied by everything from large fishing boats to catamarans.

To this day, every time we pull into the parking lot at the launch, I am filled with anticipation. There is so much excitement surrounding the endless potential of a new trip out on the big pond.

But if I'm being honest, my outlook on Lake Michigan fishing wasn't always this sunny.

During my youth, my grandparents had a boat suitable for the big water. It was hefty enough to handle the waves and provided enough space to comfortably fish with four people while running up to 12 lines out the back and sides.

When my dad would get off work, he and I often joined my Grandpa Tony and Grandma Jane as they
loaded up the old red Ford Explorer and pulled the boat to the launch in Sheboygan, located on the far east side of the city.

When I was five years old, I joined my mom, dad, grandma, and grandpa for an afternoon trip out on the lake. This is the only time I can remember the five of us being on a fishing trip together and, to this day, I cannot recall exactly why we found ourselves on my grandpa's boat. This combination of family members fishing at the same time was a rarity when I was growing up. In fact, I'm not sure I can bring to memory many, if any, other instances of the five of us gathering for an adventure out on the water.

In any event, our evening got off to a great start. We very quickly had a pair of nice rainbow trout in the boat. I can still see one of them dancing across the top of the water, splashing and flailing behind the boat as my dad reeled it in.

But Lake Michigan is a fickle creature. And, as is prone to happen from time to time, her temperament quickly changed. A thick layer of fog rolled in with almost no warning.

Keep in mind, this was before the days of advanced fish finders that were equipped with a GPS. My grandpa's boat was outfitted with little more than a compass and marine radio.

Given that we were miles from shore and could hardly see past the bow of the boat, we were lost. Plain and simple. With no line of vision, there was nothing to give us a point of reference or a sense of direction outside of the old black compass mounted to the dashboard.

We slowly made our way westward. If nothing else, we would cruise close enough to the shoreline and at least be able to get a better idea of our location.

My anxiety about the situation made me sick to my stomach.

As we puttered along, my grandpa would honk the boat horn every minute or so. The surrounding boats did the same. This audible feedback gave everyone in the vicinity an approximate idea of the number and location of the surrounding boats.

I could tell we were getting closer to shore because I began to hear the foghorn of the north pier lighthouse let out its eerie groan every once in a while.

Eventually (and mercifully), we came across a sailboat that was headed to the harbor. We followed its wake as the foghorn began to get louder.

Looking back now, it's startling to know that, somewhere in the clouds, a 55-foot bright red tower was looming. But we just couldn't see it.

A short while later, the lighthouse finally appeared just off our bow and we entered the harbor. We were finally safe.

My grandpa went to Fleet Farm the following day and purchased a handheld GPS. But I was more than a bit gun-shy about returning to the cold blue waters of Lake Michigan for several years following this incident.

Then I went through a spell where I got wickedly seasick when we were out on the lake. It's an awful feeling that I can still sense even when I'm not actively experiencing it. It feels as though nothing you do can make your stomach calm down. You're on edge, fearing that your next move might be the one that makes you vomit.

Dealing with this in front of concerned and well-intentioned family members exacerbates the problem. I've found that nothing makes you less OK than being frequently asked if you are OK. The odd pressure of knowing that seemingly everyone is keeping a close eye on you just makes your stomach feel worse.

I applaud the patience that my family showed me during this stretch. Though I'm sure it wasn't fun to deal with, the way they handled the situation was a key part of facilitating my love for fishing. I still fish Lake Michigan to this day, free of sickness, in large part because of their level of understanding when I was younger.

Grandpa Tony passed away in 2013. I have many incredible outdoor memories with him, including a boatload of them on Lake Michigan (pardon the pun). But one memory always comes to mind first.

I can't remember how old I was or what brought this topic up, though I recall exactly what my grandpa said. We were trolling around the waters on the north side of Sheboygan as the evening sun was making its way toward the western horizon. I was sitting in the passenger's seat when, looking ahead into the distance, my grandpa made an offhand comment about his own mortality. He said, "When I go, some of the fondest memories I've made in my life were on this lake."

I remember those words every single time we are on the big pond. That's when I feel closest to my grandpa. I'd like to think that's how he would have wanted it.

At my grandpa's funeral, my dad placed an orange Easter Egg spoon from Jeff's Tackle in the casket. In my grandpa's later years, that was one of the most productive lures we had on the boat and it caught us many large king salmon. We still run those spoons to this day.

My grandpa's passing was both the end of an era and a new beginning for our family's fishing adventures.

My dad now has his own boat large enough to take on the Lake Michigan waves. In some ways, I have started to transition into my dad's former role as a sort of first mate, partially in charge of getting lines in the water, netting fish, and other vital tasks. My dad is now closer to my grandpa's old position of captain, driving the boat, gathering intel, and monitoring weather conditions in the advance of our sessions. Though he is still very hands-on when it comes to setup.

Each summer, we spend time in search of salmon and trout, though probably not as much as we would like. We average about a dozen trips per season. Sometimes, that number is bolstered by our participation in a local salmon derby.

On occasion, we bring family friends along. Their reactions to even the smallest parts of the experience quickly remind me how much I've taken Lake Michigan for granted over the years, whether it's the lake breeze, the sunsets, or the feeling of near weightlessness that comes with riding along as the boat powers through the big blue waves. It's fun and enlightening to bring others on the boat, especially when they are first-timers.

These days, we generally launch out of either Sheboygan or Port Washington, about 30 miles south of our hometown.

The drop-off in water depth outside of the harbor is a little more pronounced in Port Washington than it is in Sheboygan. This can have an impact on the volatility of the water temperatures between the two locations. In a lake that has little to offer in terms of bottom structure, finding the right mix of water temperatures at different depths (also known as a thermocline) is vital.

At times, the bite can differ significantly between the two locations. We try to pick our port of choice based on a mix of fishing reports and our own recent experiences. If we're locked in on the fish in one location, we'll go there. If the going is slow, we'll give the other spot a try.

On this particular evening, in the middle of June 2020, I joined my mom and dad on an evening trip out of Port. We headed south of town as we powered out of the harbor, the

125-horsepower Mercury singing away behind my dad's Stratos. We ran nine lines out of the 19-foot red and white boat. With the kicker motor fired up, we began setting rods.

Getting the gear in the water can be a meticulous process because, to be blunt, fishing on Lake Michigan requires a lot of "stuff."

First, there are the lures. We primarily use spoons and flies, but we also have a variety of J-plugs and stick baits at our disposal.

It has been said that many lures are designed to catch fishermen, not fish. My family's collection of spoons proves this to be true.

I love shopping for spoons, as do my dad and grandma. They have fun names like Seagull Snot, Monkey Puke, Broken Taillight, and Jaeger Bomb.

As amusing as the lures may be, there is so much more to Lake Michigan fishing equipment than that.

The rods themselves are built a little tougher than the average fishing rod. What they lack in sensitivity they make up for in strength. They are meant to consistently provide the leverage needed to tackle the 10-to-20-pound fish we frequently encounter in Lake Michigan.

The open-faced reels we put on these rods are bigger too. They have plenty of capacity for the hundreds of yards of line they are each required to hold.

That amount of line may seem excessive, but it's necessary for two reasons.

First is that the powerful fish we are after can often pull out 20 or 30 yards of line at a time throughout different points of a fight. This can happen on several occasions over the course of a 10- or 15-minute battle. In order to emerge victoriously, you need to have some insurance on your reel.

The second reason is Lake Michigan's daunting size. There is a lot of water to cover out there. If you think about it, the fact that anyone is able to successfully put a five-inch lure in front of a single hungry fish in a lake that spans over 22,000 square miles is nothing short of a miracle. And in order to do that, you need lots of line.

We often fish in depths of over 100 feet. And the odds are that the fish are nowhere near our boat. So, in order to get to them, we need tools to get our lures and line to the proper depths and distances away from the boat.

There are three main pieces of equipment that help achieve this: planer boards, dipsy divers, and downriggers.

Planer boards primarily help with adding width to our presentation. These rectangular devices are constructed of foam, plastic or both and clip onto the line about 15 feet or so from the lure. They add surface tension to the line that pulls the entire setup away from the boat with the lure running a few feet below the surface.

Downriggers exclusively provide depth for our lures. These are spools filled with metal wire with an arm that extends a foot or two over the side or back of the boat.

The fishing line is attached to the metal wire with a clip that also holds a weighted ball which forces the line to the desired depth. The downrigger cable and fishing line are slowly lowered simultaneously and a counter on the downrigger shows the depth of the ball and gives an approximate depth for the corresponding lure.

It is crucial that the downrigger cable and fishing line are lowered at a slow, steady rate to avoid tangles between the two lines or a mess on the spool of the reel. This is a delicate song and dance, especially when the water is a bit bumpy.

When trolling, the rods attached to the downrigger have a

bend in them as though there is a fish on. When a fish strikes, the pressure usually pulls the line off the clip and the rod stands straight up. With a less aggressive bite, the rod tip may begin pounding up or down, but remain bent. This typically means the line is still attached to the release clip on the cable.

Finally, there are dipsy divers. These plastic discs provide the best of both worlds. They add depth to the presentation, while also getting the lure away from the boat. A dial on the back of the device allows the user to select the angle the bait should run in hopes of creating a combination of the ideal depth and width.

Our preferred setup utilizes all three of these tools to create a presentation that would look like a "v," if viewed from the back of the boat.

The planer boards run closest to the surface on the outsides of the boat. Next, come the dipsy divers that run at a medium depth off each corner of the back of the boat. The downriggers are in the middle of the back of the boat running straight down at the maximum depth of any lures in our spread.

On this day, our two downriggers were double-stacked, each forcing a pair of lures to our desired depth. A trio of dipsy diver rods got their baits to a medium depth and out away from the boat. Lines fitted with planer boards flanked each side of the setup, adding width to our presentation.

Using these methods allows us to span several depths and cover as much territory as possible. This is crucial because, with little cover at the bottom of the lake, the fish gravitate toward the water that is either at their preferred temperature or that of the food they are pursuing.

There are some pretty nifty pieces of equipment to help anglers assess the water temperature below the surface. They are called Fish Hawks and we have owned a pair of these in different styles. Both models clip onto lines or downrigger cables.

One version provides feedback on the water temperature at different depths in real time. The version my dad owned at the time was lowered and then retrieved, so the information can be deciphered at the surface. It can be a time-consuming process, especially if you are checking frequently. So we used this tool sparingly.

We overcame the lack of timely data by spreading out our presentation across as much of the water column as possible. The approach works for us, but my dad is jonesing for one of the more advanced models. Information is your friend when you are trying to have a fish bite your tiny lure in the vast expanse of one of America's largest freshwater lakes.

Generally, it takes a bit of time for the fishing to pick up in the evenings. Getting fish early can be a sign that you are catching the last of the feeding window. In my experience, you are often in for a slow night if you catch a fish right away.

With lines in the water, we opened the soft-sided cooler and enjoyed dinner, our traditional sandwiches made with Johnsonville summer sausage and whatever cheese was in the fridge tucked between sliced and buttered Sheboygan hard rolls.

Whether we were out on the water well before dawn or enjoying the last of the daylight the sun has to offer, I cannot think of a trip on Lake Michigan with my family that didn't include these sandwiches.

Just enough time passed before one of the downrigger rods began to dance. My dad grabbed the rod and handed it to my mom. We were hooked up. I grabbed the net and waited for my chance to step in and help finish the deal.

With the fish nearing the end of the line, literally and

figuratively, my mom took a handful of steps toward the bow of the boat. I took her place and scooped the fish from the cold blue water. It was a medium king salmon.

We were on the board. As my grandpa frequently said, "That's the main thing."

There's a sense of relief that comes with not getting skunked, no matter how good you think you are.

Next, it was my turn. The drag on one of the board rods began screaming. As I ran to it, I could see that a display of aerial acrobatics was already underway. That could only mean one thing: a rainbow trout was stuck on those hooks. They are feisty fish, by far the most athletic of the Lake Michigan salmon and trout species.

I started in on the couple hundred yards of line that separated me and the fish. Mom took the wheel as dad gave instructions to both of us. Fishing out here is the definition of a team effort. It takes a village. With a group this small, no one is allowed to sit by idly when a fish is on the line.

Standing at the bow, I began to make headway. The orange planer board made its way to the side of the boat. My dad had to scoop and disconnect it while I did my best to maintain pressure on the fish. These are always tense moments, but it is part of the game.

With the board successfully released, it was just me and the fish. A short while later, the rainbow was in the net. We were two-for-two.

Before I knew it, we were on again. My mom got this one, and the way the fish was fighting made it seem big. A quick glimpse as the fish's dorsal fin broke the surface in the distance increased the evidence. I steered the boat as my dad coached my mom through the fight.

After some time passed, the fish began to tire and reluctantly approached the rail. My dad went down with the net, but the fish didn't want to cooperate. It mustered up the strength for another small run away from the boat.

My mom once again gained the upper hand. Time for Take 2. This time, my dad managed to get the fish into the net and onto the floor of the boat.

The fish was indeed on the larger side. A solid king, probably three years old with a weight somewhere near 17 or 18 pounds. It had survived three-quarters of its maximum lifespan before finding its way into our boat.

My second at-bat came about in short succession. Another strike on a board rod produced a second rainbow, this one almost identical in size to the first. And, like that one, it was placed in the cooler.

Next, it was time to get my dad in on the action. He is always the first one to give up a rod to someone else. His main concern is that someone on his boat catches a fish and, while he certainly loves catching them as much as anyone, he often seems indifferent about who gets to accomplish the feat.

One of the downrigger rods sprung to life and my mom and I insisted that my dad pick it up. He strong-armed the solid fish to the boat – our first lake trout of the night. These fish inhabit some of the lake's coldest water. Lakers are capable of thriving in temperatures hovering just above freezing. The layers of body fat required to make this a reality often make laker meat greasy, and for some anglers it's less than desirable. The way I see it, the fat that runs through their flesh makes lake trout ideal candidates for the smoker. I think of those morsels as a type of thick-cut fish bacon.

The fish had just made its way to the cooler when one of the dipsy diver rods bent in half and stayed pinned there. My dad was closest, so he scooped the rod. The noise of drag filled the air as my dad began to strain. This wasn't your average fish.

While many fishermen have been known to embellish on occasion, my dad has caught enough fish to know when the one he's fighting is truly in the upper echelon. When he says it's big, I'm inclined to believe him.

The battle persisted. My dad continued to finesse the fish while maintaining adequate pressure. Then, suddenly, the rod went limp. The tension was gone. The fish managed to elude us, turning into the proverbial "one that got away." Even with five fish in the boat, this missed chance stung.

My dad and I often discuss, only half-jokingly, how we could catch 100 fish in a day and we would still spend too much time thinking about how we lost No. 101.

No matter how many fish you pull in, losing one still stings. How long that feeling lingers is dependent on the situation. In instances when we come home with a bunch of fish and just happen to have one come loose, the sensation of disappointment will often be brushed off in a matter of hours. But if things were slow or the fish that wiggled off the hook was large, as it was on this night, we often find ourselves continuing to discuss our misfortune for days. By my estimation, that is simply an innate part of an angler's mentality.

It's been a long time since the feeling of losing a fish lingered as much as it did that night. Though another unfortunate experience will inevitably come along to take its place. If you fish long enough, you learn this is a certainty.

At this point, we had five fish on six hits. All of this had occurred in a little more than an hour.

The flurry of action left our setup in disarray. Many of our lines weren't in the water but were instead strewn about the boat. Some were tangled while others needed to be re-tied for a variety of reasons. This has a way of happening on the big pond. At least there were fish to show for all of the chaos. We needed to regroup and we took a few moments to do just that.

Everything was back in the water just in time for the golden hour, which is the 30 minutes prior to sunset and the half-hour after. We collected another laker and a coho salmon in that span.

The night concluded with seven fish in the box: two kings, two lakers, two rainbows, and a coho. We were just a brown trout short of the Lake Michigan Grand Slam.

Every night, there seems to be at least one group that strolls up to the cleaning station and unloads a cooler full of big fish. While it doesn't happen to us often, it was nice to be able to take our turn being those people.

On the ride home, my dad called my grandma and put her on speakerphone through the truck's Bluetooth.

"You caught HOW many?" she asked in excitement. "I don't think we ever came home with that many with dad."

That sentiment meant a lot to me. It nearly brought a tear to my eye. And, as I look back, she was mostly right. My dad and I caught nine cohos on a night trip to Port a few years back. But this particular trip stood as one of the most successful we had ever had on Lake Michigan and that is saying something given my family's history on this body of water.

Grandpa would have been proud.

CHAPTER 5

Carp Fishing

Fish Nos. 24-25

Carp seem to have an image problem. Many anglers feel they are a "garbage fish" and, while I can't speak for everyone who enjoys fishing, there are a few likely reasons for this.

The first is that carp are classified by the Wisconsin DNR and many wildlife agencies around the country as "rough fish." The very definition of that term is "a usually freshwater fish (such as a buffalo or freshwater drum) considered undesirable as a food or sport fish and often viewed as a competitor of more desirable fishes." But it is tough to tell if the reputation of carp is shaped by this definition or if the definition was shaped by the reputation. In either case, there is a real chance confirmation bias plays a role.

Carp are bottom feeders and, for some people, that fact alone conjures up images of fish ingesting mud and pollution. This is enough for these fish to have a bad rap in the eyes of some. Though, as I think about it, equating bottom-feeding fish to meat that is not desirable or even unsafe to eat seems like it could have more to do with how humans treat the environment than an inherent problem with carp biology. It doesn't need to be an assumption that the bottom of every water body is riddled with toxins.

Now, I will grant that carp are less than ideal table fare. I've both fried and baked filets. Both of these culinary adventures yielded results that were mushy in texture with a flavor that had a hint of mud to it. Not exactly ideal dining.

But this is hardly a reason to dismiss carp as a desirable fish to target. In my opinion, those who do are missing out.

The common carp is one of my favorite fish to catch. Pound for pound, carp fight harder than nearly any fish I have encountered, second only to king salmon or perhaps an angry northern pike.

This was showcased during a time I went fishing with a friend on the Mullet River at Anton Park in Plymouth when I was in middle school.

The term "park" is used loosely in this instance. Just beyond a parking lot is a walking path that leads to downtown. On the other side of that path is a strip of grass that is about 30 yards long by 10 yards wide. A small dam controls the flow of a millpond into a narrow stretch of river below. From there, the river makes a straight shot to the traffic bridge.

On sunny days, I would venture to the sidewalk on the traffic bridge and spy on the carp that were going about their business in the river. It was commonplace to see a dozen carp methodically cruising upstream as they inhaled anything they found desirable on the bottom.

Every once in a while, those desirable things would be the baits on the end of my hook.

On one long-ago day, a hungry carp tugged on my line so hard that it ripped the pole out of my hastily-constructed rod holder and into the water. To say my teenage self was panicked is an understatement. The rod wasn't even mine. It was hard to enjoy the fishing while I anticipated the lecture that awaited me when I got home.

But an hour later, my friend Alistar caught the same fish, hook in mouth, yards from where I had hooked up. It was still dragging my dad's spinning rod along for the ride. If I had been old enough to legally do so, I would have gone home and bought a lottery ticket that day.

In my part of the world, carp are available in abundance. Most significant water sources in the area have carp and many of them hold large ones.

Pursuing carp is about as simple as it gets from a technique and equipment standpoint. I once read a quote in a Field and Stream article that said carp fishing is "like dragging a piece of fried chicken through the local seniors' center. If it looks good and moves slowly enough, something will eventually try to gum it to death."

Though this particular piece was referring to fly fishing for carp, a lot of the same principles apply to spinning reel setups.

These bottom feeders will slurp down a nightcrawler, nibble on kernels of corn, or chow down on homemade dough balls. They even vacuum up flies on occasion. In my experience, the two keys to carp fishing success are to keep your bait stationary and bring it to the fish's eye level. Sure, you can score a few of these fish with a bait that sits directly on the bottom, but in my experience, keeping it a few inches above increases the intrigue for the fish.

Hot summer nights are my favorite time to go after carp. I've had some success in spring and, this year, even managed to continue scoring commons well into October. But summer is, no doubt, the prime time. Many local rivers begin to shallow out. This greatly reduces current. More slack water usually means more carp, where I'm from.

It was the night after the Fourth of July and temperatures had been in the 80s for much of the week, with plentiful sunshine. My wife Lyza decided to join me on this trip.

I've known Lyza since fourth grade. For most of that time, I had a crush on her. But we didn't start dating until shortly after we graduated high school. I like to joke that we made up for lost time because, within a year of dating, we both chose to transfer to UW-Stevens Point to complete our degrees. Shortly after we graduated, we got married.

If I had to put a number to it, I would say Lyza and I fish together about 10 times a year. Sometimes she fishes. Other times she reads a book while enjoying the sunshine and fresh air.

Though she doesn't always actively participate in our fishing adventures, make no mistake, Lyza can hold her own as an angler. She is patient and a fast learner.

When we were dating, I would often fish the Sheboygan River behind her parent's house, where I fished on the Opening Day of this season. Every once in a while, she would grab a pole and join me. On more than one occasion, she has caught more or larger fish than I did.

Selfishly, I also appreciate her willingness to take her own fish off the hook. It saves me precious fishing time.

On our yearly family trip to Vilas County, Lyza will be alongside my parents and me as we fish for walleye or panfish.

She has always been very understanding of the time I dedicate to fishing, and it means a lot to me that Lyza also possesses firsthand knowledge of angling. She gets it at a level that wouldn't be possible if she herself hadn't spent time fishing. It's amazing to be married to someone who has an intimate knowledge of one of my foremost passions.

Our July 5 trip didn't start out as a carp venture; in fact, I was trying to sneak off to Jetzer Lake outside of neighboring Howards Grove. The small lake, which is more of a large pond, produces some solid bass. As an added bonus, there is a spacious dock that allows shore anglers like me to get in on the action.

As Lyza and I rolled up to the parking lot on this muggy summer evening, we encountered a familiar issue. The dock was full of people who had beaten us to the punch. With no real room to fish, we decided to move on.

I have a love/hate relationship with fishing pressure. On the one hand, it's great to see people out enjoying the outdoors, especially when they have children along with them. After all, we only protect what we understand and there is no better way to understand nature than to become an active participant in it.

On the flip side, the natural competitor in me was peeved I couldn't give my desired spot a try. Especially when I spent 30 minutes of my limited fishing time traveling to and from the location.

It was off to a secondary spot. I had nightcrawlers and could easily convert my spinning rods from bass to carp setups. The conditions seemed right, so we headed for River Park in downtown Sheboygan Falls and the familiar banks of the Sheboygan River.

We still had over two hours until it got properly dark and I was optimistic about our chances as I began to set the lines. I know this stretch of the river well. Nestled between two of the park's footbridges, it contains what remained of the weeping willows that used to dominate this stretch of shoreline, and my Grandma Ruth's old house is just across the river. When my mom was a kid, she used to join her dad and her siblings Dan, Tim, and Debby on a dock placed there by my late Grandpa Wally. The family would enjoy evenings on the river fishing with cane poles and corn. Bullhead were plentiful, but carp would also make their way into the mix on occasion. The children would place some of the carp in an old metal washtub filled with water and feed them soda crackers.

Growing up, I spent many a summer afternoon on that riverbank with my grandpa, using those same cane poles. The dock was long gone, but we sat on a red plaid picnic blanket. Corn was always the bait of choice in his eyes. He emptied cans of bright yellow kernels into an empty olive-colored Country Crock butter container. This provided us with a lid for our bait and helped make clear to anyone who opened the fridge that this corn was for fishing, not human consumption.

Though it's not a method I lean on heavily anymore, we still caught plenty of fish with the vegetable approach. Panfish and bullhead were the main participants. My grandpa always had an old rag on hand to help him navigate the bony barbs of the small bullhead when I was too young to take the fish off the hook myself.

During a couple of winters, I ice-fished this stretch of river.

Once when I couldn't have been older than 12, my Uncle Tim joined me on the river. Though he didn't have much fishing experience, I convinced him to come along and keep me company. All we had was a blue hand auger with dull blades, three tip-ups, and a bucket of minnows.

We ultimately resorted to using the sharp blade atop the handle of our ice skimmer to chip away at the thinner ice in some previously used holes. We didn't have any luck that day. But I still hold this memory dear because it is one of the only times I have ever gone fishing with my uncle.

One Christmas, when I was in my early 20s, my dad and I decided to place some tip-ups in the middle of the river. Once the lines were set, we retreated to the warmth of my grandma's house and observed from the back window as we opened presents and enjoyed plenty of food and drink. When a fish struck, an orange flag would pop up and alert us to the bite.

About an hour later, I looked out the window and saw a flag blowing in the breeze. Like firefighters hopping out of bed for a late-night call, my dad and I ran to the front door, slipped on our boots and coats and quickly made our way through the backyard and down the hill to the river.

When we arrived at the tip-up, the spool was spinning. So we knew the fish was still hooked. I let my dad have the honor of grabbing the line and setting the hook. When he felt the full force of the fish, he looked up at me and said, "This feels like a nice one."

And it was. A few minutes later, a 27-inch northern pike emerged from the hole. It wasn't a monster. But it was by far the largest pike I had seen pulled out of this part of the river.

We took a few pictures and sent the fish back on its way.

My dad and I reset the tip-up with some fresh bait and returned to the house to continue enjoying some old-fashioneds and munching chicken puffs and cold ham that my uncle had grilled the day before.

We didn't get any more bites that day. But we got our money's worth from the one fish we did catch.

Without fail, I think about these things every time I fish this spot across the river.

By early 2020, things had changed. Prior to opening day, my wife and I went to scout the bank by my grandma's house. The home would soon be put up for sale since my grandma had transitioned to assisted living. I was hoping to find a way to fish this overgrown shore at least one more time, for old times' sake.

But we quickly discovered that the river had evolved significantly since I last fished this spot, well over a decade ago. I'm not sure why I had waited so long to give this spot another look. Surely, this place would have been fishable at some point over the last 10 years. But today's situation and my feelings of nostalgia had me kicking myself for taking those opportunities for granted.

A shallow silty layer stretched nearly 10 yards into the river, with far too little water to hold any fish. The lengthy willow branches made casting into the middle of the river nearly impossible. This was starting to look like a pipe dream.

I had opted against fishing there on opening day, but I still toyed with the idea of making it work before the house was sold.

While that thought was still clunking around my brain, Lyza and I began the setup process. I discovered a more immediate and pressing issue: I didn't have a rod holder with me. I was originally planning to cast for bass, so I didn't come equipped with all of the necessary tools for deadsticking.

So I gently rested my rods against the back of my tackle box. Certainly, this was tempting fate given some of my previous incidents, but I didn't have many other options at the moment.

The action popped off in a hurry. It was only a few minutes before I found myself scurrying toward a rod that was being pulled in the general direction of the river. The silver reel banged against the side of the tackle box as the black rod tried to make its way into the stained water. I grabbed the rod before it could escape my grasp. I set the hook and a reddish-orange tail burst through the water's surface. The carp were hungry.

After a minor struggle, I brought the fish ashore. It was on the small side of medium, but the fight was enjoyable. Any frustration I had from not being able to fish Jetzer Lake quickly evaporated. It was clear we were on the fish and we still had plenty of time.

A short while later, I was gazing off into the distance when I was forced back into reality by Lyza's yelling, "Nathan!" as she pointed toward a rod that was doubled over.

"You get this one," I hollered back to her. She ran over to the rod from her spot a few yards to the left, reeled up the slack and pulled. The splashing that ensued answered any questions surrounding whether she had connected.

As the fish came closer to shore, Lyza had to direct it around a large branch that pointed out of the water. This stick was a known hazard. Earlier in the season, I encountered a similar situation in a carp battle of my own. My line got tangled in the timber with the fish still attached to the hook. I was forced to ditch my socks and shoes and wade out about 10 yards to free the line, only to have it snap and the fish swim away. It was then I realized I was up to my knees in muck.

Fortunately, we were able to avoid a similar scene this time around. We landed the fish, but Lyza opted out of the picture-taking opportunity.

The relatively dry conditions made the water near shore extremely shallow. There was so little water that the mucky bottom was visible between the gaps of the patches of green lily pads. Many of the fish I had caught in the past became beached before ever making it to land, causing me to go on several rescue missions.

A previous trip resulted in a need for new footwear. I ventured into the river and both legs became completely stuck, immobilized by the suction-like force of the muddy bottom.

Without anything to grasp for leverage, I slowly began twisting and shifting in an effort to free myself. When I eventually became dislodged from the unrelenting grip, I was missing one of my Crocs. It was consumed by the muck monster, never to be seen again. I fished the rest of that night down one shoe.

Given these circumstances, releasing the fish became its own obstacle. In these conditions, fish often can't be placed back in the exact spot they came from. In the past, I have either had to walk downshore in hopes of finding deeper waters that allowed the fish to swim away without effort or would wade in to find the depth I was looking for.

Today, I opted for the latter, not wanting to be too far from my active rods. I released Lyza's fish and climbed back on dry land.

"You're covered in mud," my wife observed with a chuckle, stating the obvious as though to point out she empathized with my situation.

"I know," I said through a smile. "But I don't care. This is awesome."

I was euphoric. The action was hot and we were catching one of my favorite species. In short order, we already had two between the both of us. I was in my happy place and Lyza and I were both enjoying it.

Not every carp strike is alike. Nothing gets my blood rushing like seeing a rod tip just pounding as it's converted into a backward C shape. But these large fish can sometimes be surprisingly subtle, particularly when they don't know they're hooked.

I was scanning our lineup of rods when I noticed an unusual amount of slack on one of the lines. The rod sat completely still, but the limp line was slowly moving. There was a fish on the other end and it was swimming toward us.

After a few cranks of the reel, I gave a tug. Instant weight. This fish had shoulders. It darted against the current, now fully aware of its predicament. The drag began to sing. In my head, this fish was far from on the scoreboard.

The good news was the fish made its move in the direction of the deeper water, minimizing the chances it would become prematurely beached. The bad news? It now had the full potential of its power at its disposal and it was putting it to use.

It felt like a pretty good hook job, but I continued to fight carefully, yet confidently. We were about 10 minutes in when the carp took a hard left and swam with the current. It was now in shallower depths and this had the potential to become problematic.

A few yards away, a father/son duo was fishing the adjacent lagoon. The pair started to make their way over to us amid the commotion. They were naturally curious and hoped to see the result of this matchup.

I muscled the fish closer to shore, but was running out of water. The fish was laboring without its natural protection, but so was I. As mud began to cover the carp, it gained additional weight. The friction brought forth by the relentless muck added strain to the line and I grew concerned about how this could end. This was certainly to the fish's advantage.

As the fish drew nearer, the child (I placed him at about 7 or 8 years old) left his dad's side and wandered toward the water. He had a net with a short silver shaft and green braided thread. He was woefully underequipped. There was no way this net was up to the task. But I appreciated his willingness to assist me and wasn't about to tell him no. He just wanted to help and be part of the action.

Still connected to the line, the fish was now fully stuck in the mud a few feet from shore. The kid reached as far as his small arms would allow and somehow managed to get the tiny net around the fish's head. The carp sat parked in the mud, half its sizable body in the net, half of it out.

The child went for the scoop and, as he lifted, the fish fought its way out and back into the mud. It was closer to shore than where it was initially captured, but not yet on land. It was at this point the child handed the net to me.

I took a different approach. I slid the net under the fish's tail and used it to guide the mouth toward me. I managed to get something of a grip on the slippery, mud-covered carp, hoisting the fish to shore. It was over. Everything that needed to go our way did.

After I extended a couple of thank yous, the father and son were on their way. I unhooked the fish, got some measurements and took a few pictures. If you don't have a scale handy, you can approximate a carp's weight by taking its length (in inches) and dividing it by four. By this measure, the fish was probably about 8 pounds. By this unofficial measurement, it was my largest of the season.

The pleasantly warm evening wore on and my wife and I continued to fish. We got a few more bites but, as it seemingly always does, the action began to taper off as darkness set in.

We spent the remainder of our time enjoying each other's company and the success we shared together. There's something powerful about sharing an activity I love with the person I love most and this was a moment I savored.

CHAPTER 6

Pounds, Not Inches

Fish No. 28

Bass fishing is one of the most popular types of angling in America. According to a study published by the National Survey of Fishing, nearly 36 million people over the age of 16 went fishing in 2016 and bass were the most popular target species.

It's easy to see why so many people are fans of bass fishing. Bass are distributed widely across the country and can be found in each of the lower 48 states. These aggressive, hard-fighting fish are fun to catch and not hard to find. In fact, smallmouth and largemouth bass made up over 72 percent of the fish I caught during this particular season.

Bass are the ideal species for the weekend warrior. To me, they sit at the perfect intersection of entertainment and effort. They aren't as easy to find as panfish, but are generally much larger and more fun to catch. Yet it's easier to convince a bass to bite your bait than a muskie.

Sure, like any fish, you have to work for them on occasion, but if Saturday is your only day to hit the water you still have a fighting chance at finding enough willing participants to put together an enjoyable day.

The same can't be said of all species—for instance, salmon and trout on Lake Michigan. Staying on the salmon bite often requires plenty of advanced technology and intimate knowledge of the changing weather and water conditions.

While this can also be true for bass, the average person stands a much better chance of finding consistent success with old-school tactics and limited technology. Heck, I don't even need a boat to go bass fishing.

Bass are truly a fish for the people.

This particular brand of fishing also enjoys substantial marketing and public relations support, unlike any other discipline. Nearly all televised fishing tournaments are bass events.

One of the most popular tournament series, Bassmaster, is backed by the Bass Anglers Sportsman Society (B.A.S.S.), which boasts over 20,000 members.

There aren't many proper celebrities in the world of fishing, but nearly all of the few who exist are bass anglers.

Countless websites and brands have built digital empires around the species and social media platforms are flooded with communities and posts dedicated to the pursuit of bass. There are good reasons for this popularity. Bass are plentiful in much of the country. They are fun to catch and provide many people a pathway into the angling world.

I've caught plenty of bass in my life, but I haven't ever considered myself a "bass fisherman" per se. Where I live, bass are just around. You can easily catch them from shore and it's an enjoyable way to spend time. Sure, I target them specifically many times. But if other species were available in such numbers, I'd probably spend time pursuing those instead.

This year, I decided to be more intentional about my quest for bass. I figured that if I was going to spend so much time fishing for them, I might as well hone the craft and get better at catching larger ones. The process of continuous learning paired with the opportunity to improve my skill set are two of the things I find most appealing about fishing.

One of my college roommates, JT, is an excellent bass fisherman. But, for whatever reason, we didn't fish together very often in college. Our initial bond was forged on our senses of humor and our love of hockey. However, fishing has been one of the primary threads that have kept us close since graduation.

Looking back, I regret not spending more time fishing with JT in college. But I hope to make up for the lost time in the years to come.

JT and I exchange text messages almost daily and fishing is one of the most popular topics of discussion. Any time he sends me a fish picture from his family's cabin on Potato Lake in Minnesota, he always tells me what the fish weighed, not how long it was. I remain jealous of the sheer size of the bass he catches. Early in the season, I made the decision that I wanted to start catching bass like that.

Easier said than done, especially when shore fishing is your primary method. As they say, "That's why they call it 'fishing,' not 'catching.'" That's especially true in my case.

I began by increasing my stockpile of bass lures. I started with what I knew: Senkos, spinners, and stick baits. Eventually, I graduated to swimbaits and floating frogs. I began to reassess my list of spots with a fresh perspective while also scouting out new locations. I read articles about new methods and tactics and, eventually, began the pursuit of my own fish I could measure in pounds.

It was slow going at first. There were plenty of days I came home and entered a nice, fat zero in my fishing log. But every trip brought added knowledge and I could feel myself making progress, even if I didn't have the fish count to show for it. If nothing else, I had learned a lot about what not to do.

I tested every potential variable that came to mind. Bait types, casting distances and angles, locations, times of day, retrieval speed, anything I could think of. I would spend my time off the water concocting different hypotheses and would then head to a lake or river and test them. These experiments helped me cross theories off my mental checklist.

For better or worse, I began to tighten my focus on a particular set of spots that I felt gave me a fighting chance. One of those spots was an inland location called Woodlake, in the village of Kohler, just down the road from my house. The 21-acre waterway is nestled behind what amounts to a high-end strip mall with a market, hotel, and restaurants. This beautiful glorified pond is a well-known bass spot frequented by local anglers. A gravel walking path circles the lake and provides incredible ease of access. Its clear waters readily showcase the numerous large bass that live there. But these fish are highly pressured.

Woodlake is another one of those spots that's easy access and relatively consistent fishing can make it a bit busy at times, which is both a good and a bad thing. On the one hand, it's great to see people enjoying the sport I love. Folks need a place to fish and accessible, reliable spots are a great way to keep the general public interested in fishing. This, in turn, leads to sustainable or increased license sales and, ideally, a deeper appreciation of the outdoors among our populace. The numerous benefits of that certainly outweigh my desire to fish in peace.

Fellow anglers can also be a great source of knowledge, whether through conversation or observation. It's amazing what you can learn if you just ask or are willing to shut up and watch what's going on around you. I can't tell you how many times a nearby group is out fishing near me when I quietly pull out several fish from a spot on the same body of water. Focused on their own little world, they become frustrated by their lack of results and simply leave. But some simple observation would have given them a new set of information to reevaluate their location and tactics, whether on that day or a future trip. For that reason, I try to always be aware of my surroundings without diverting too much attention from the task at hand.

But, the way I see it, there are two downsides to fishing pressure. One is that there are only so many quality spots to go around, especially when you are fishing from shore. With your options already limited to what you can effectively fish from the bank, your prospects narrow when other anglers enter the picture.

The second is that an abundance of fishing pressure can quickly make fish wary. These "educated fish" are much harder to entice. They are by no means impossible to catch, but your success rate relies upon fishing at the proper times and occasionally presenting baits in a more accurate or non-traditional way. This shrinks the already unforgivingly thin margin of error.

Even with all of this taken into account, I decided Woodlake was one of the better choices I had on the table. So I began to put my time in. My first four trips resulted in skunks. Part of this was due to the natural learning curve that comes with any new location.

One of those fruitless trips was with my co-worker Trevor.

At this time, we had worked together at The Vollrath Company in Sheboygan for a couple of years as members of the digital marketing team. He sits in a cubical next to mine and we quickly bonded over our love of sports.

Trevor is friendly and incredibly easy to talk to. He is intelligent, well-rounded, and a great listener who has an astonishing ability to retain information. He self-identifies as an introvert, but I have never known him to be afraid to strike up a conversation with anyone. We have spent many afternoons in the office locked in wide-ranging conversations that attempt to tackle both work and life.

One day, the subject of fishing came up and I discovered that Trevor was also an angling enthusiast. Though on the surface he didn't strike me as someone who would spend time wetting a thread, he told me that he chases northern pike with his family in Door County every summer and really enjoys it.

Fishing together quickly became a goal of ours and we were finally able to make it happen one June day. Both of us had been working from home for several months due to the pandemic and we figured this was a relatively safe way to spend some time together in person.

We met in the parking lot of one of the shops that dot the near side of the lake one sunny afternoon after work. Trevor showed off his impressive collection of lures and walked me through some of his favorites as the summer sun beat down on the blacktop.

The next few hours were spent casting our baits in various spots around the dry gravel walking path as we caught up on our lives and made effortless small talk on a variety of topics.

It's always fun to fish with someone for the first time. Even in the most familiar of spots, you can learn a lot through the perspective and approach of someone else. We tossed an assortment of spoons, spinners, and plastics to no avail. We engaged in several wide-ranging conversations, trading fishing stories, catching up on the latest happenings at work and learning more about each other's families.

At one point, Trevor's lure became lodged in a downed log that stretched into a nearby drop-off. He took a short swimming trip to retrieve it. Given the high temperatures, I had half a mind to join him as he plunged into cooler blue water just across the channel from me. But I settled for buying myself a lemonade once the night concluded.

We parted ways as the sun went down. Neither of us had landed a fish, though we encountered some large bass cruising the shoreline. It was still a fun night. I hadn't seen Trevor in person since March. It was nice to enjoy the company of a friend, an experience I didn't get to have often these days. Other than my initial ice fishing excursion, this was the first fishing session I had that featured a partner other than my parents or wife. But I continued to feel the pressure of getting this monkey off my back and ending my cold streak.

After giving it some more thought, I realized the other issue at play in my lack of success here was the lack of natural vegetation. It was late spring, but the temperatures hadn't regularly risen high enough to promote the growth of the large weed beds that held critical food sources to draw bass closer to shore.

Once the bottom began to get green, the tides began to turn in my favor. In early July, my dad joined me on an evening trip to Woodlake. He busted out a classic lure: the Rapala F7. It was black and silver with a subtle wiggle that perfectly mimicked a scurrying minnow. A few casts in and he had already landed a pair of largemouth bass. Even the bluegill were giving chase to the approachable bait. He ended the night with three largemouth and sunfish.

A few days later, I decided to steal a page from my dad's playbook. I also opted for the Rapala. However, it still didn't yield any results. That changed on my next trip.

It was a sunny July evening and I wanted to get outside and enjoy it. I decided to go back to Kohler and give the Rapala a college try. It took a while, but I eventually landed my first fish near the old footbridge. A modest largemouth, It was hanging out in the rocky shoreline near a significant drop-off. It felt good to be back in the win column and it gave me the mental boost I needed to keep going.

I eventually worked my way downshore toward a rock pile that gradually eased into the beginning of the dropoff I was fishing prior. I tossed my lure at a 45-degree angle to my right, landing it in the deeper water and swimming it back across the edge of the rocks. The sun had set a few minutes earlier, but the bite was still on. I saw a flash and immediately felt the pressure. I set the hook and was in business.

It was a brief but intense struggle. I brought the fish onto land and it was exactly what I had been after.

The fish measured about 18 inches and a bit over two pounds. It was the biggest largemouth bass of my life.

After grabbing my pliers, I unhooked the fish. It managed to consume five of the six hooks that hung from the belly of the bait. I snapped a few pictures and sent the fish back on its way.

The first text message went to JT... Finally, a bass I could measure in pounds, not inches.

CHAPTER 7

Fly Fishing and Friendship

Fish Nos. 40-41

Fly fishing is the bow hunting of angling. There's just an element of sophistication that comes with it. You show me someone who is proficient in fly fishing and I will show you a person who knows more about the outdoors than the average human.

When pursuing fish with a fly, particularly trout and salmon, an angler needs a certain amount of understanding about nature. There's a specific collection of abilities that require being in tune with your surroundings.

Fly fishing is all about a natural presentation. Achieving this without competency in the outdoors is nearly impossible.

First and foremost, you have to know the species you are targeting inside and out. When do they feed? How do they feed? What type of habitat do they prefer?

Then there's the entomology. What's hatching right now? What phase of their lifespan are these bugs in? How do they behave near the water? Do the fish I'm after even eat these?

I'm fairly convinced no one has ever lucked their way into consistent fly fishing success.

I will be the first to admit I don't consider myself a proper fly fishing angler. I own a fly rod—a trusty old bargain combo from the local Fleet Farm. I even use it once in a while. But it's not something I list in the "skills" section of my fishing resume. The vast majority of the fish I've caught on a fly rod consisted of foolish bass that were ready to hammer the first thing they saw, and that first thing just so happened to be my fly.

Fighting fish, even small ones, on a fly rod is a blast. In high school, I managed to land a carp on a fly rod. It was one of the most memorable fights of my fishing career and, to this day, one of my proudest outdoor accomplishments.

Once in a great while, I'm smart enough to try and take advantage of the wonderful inland trout fishing available in my part of the state.

Back in my newspaper days, I formed a friendship with Jordan, one of my co-workers.

Jordan and I quickly bonded during my early days at the Manitowoc Herald Times Reporter, the small daily publication that employed me after I graduated college in the summer of 2013. I was a sports reporter and Jordan was a digital desk producer.

We had a few things going for us: we were close in age, our desks were adjacent to each other, and we worked many of the same shifts, including lonely Saturday mornings when the skeleton crew of only two or three people had to put together a Sunday paper before 2 p.m. while the rest of our co-workers presumably enjoyed a leisurely weekend morning.

His intelligence, wit, and wide array of interests made Jordan easy to talk with and relate to. We often discussed our love of cooking and our feelings on the world around us. We commiserated about the challenges that came with being young professionals in the shifting world of media and often served as outlets for one another when things got tough.

Jordan had never been fly fishing before, but he gave it a shot. He is always willing to try something new that may enrich his life and he's not willing to let the potential of failure get in the way of expanding his horizons. For instance, when I first met Jordan, he decided to dive headfirst into the world of cooking. He would often share tales of his latest recipe experiments, both the triumphs and the disappointments.

Jordan just wants to learn from his experiences and enjoy partaking in something he's not familiar with. These are some of the things I love most about him.

One day, Jordan brought up the idea of fly fishing together.

I'm always down for a good outdoor adventure, especially with friends. This was an easy yes. We spent an enjoyable morning together on the Onion River in pursuit of brown trout.

Though I must admit I can't bring many of the specifics of that first shared adventure to mind, I remember many of the feelings.

To this day, I can still feel the warmth of the sunlight that filtered through the treetops. I can sense the unique pressure that hit my legs when the cool water came into contact with the outside of my waders as we slipped into the thin river as quietly as possible. And I can sense the excitement that jolted through my body when we spotted the first fish of the day floating lazily in the current.

In the spring of 2015, as part of an organizational restructuring, I took a sports reporter job at the Sheboygan Press, another daily paper owned by Gannett, the parent company of the Herald Times Reporter.

Jordan took on a new role within the company as a producer, a role he still holds to this day.

As we transitioned to our new positions, I missed my daily conversations with Jordan. But we managed to keep in touch periodically through text messages or Snapchat exchanges of our latest kitchen creations, even after I left the paper in mid-2015 in favor of a new career in marketing, an endeavor that continues to play into my penchant for storytelling.

This season, nearly five years after our last shift together, Jordan reached out again. He had the itch to give fly fishing another run and he was wondering if I knew of any spots.

Quick research on the Department of Natural Resources website pointed us in the direction of LaBudde Creek, a narrow stretch of water in the western part of Sheboygan County. According to the most recent stocking data, this place held more catchable brook trout than any other spot in the region.

We selected a date in mid-July that aligned with both of our schedules and decided to meet at a bridge near some public hunting land I spent some time on in the months before. My plan was to use the land as an access point to a fishable stretch of the creek. Thick underbrush surrounding the water meant that wading might be necessary but, given the narrow nature of the stream, it wasn't the desired tactic. Finding a spot conducive to casting a fly line proved to be a challenge.

Not long after we disembarked from our vehicles, I realized that I hadn't properly stressed to Jordan that waders would likely be needed. This was a foolish assumption on my part because, when we last fished together, much of the river was accessible from shore. The mature hardwoods provided ample space for casting from the banks. But this new location was a different animal. Marshy, harsh underbrush guarded the water and, as we ventured in, it quickly became clear that we would have to wade.

To his credit, Jordan's attire showed he was prepared to get a little wet. But his sandals and shorts were inadequate for the swampy terrain we were about to encounter. (If there was any doubt, the pictures of his scarred legs I received the next day confirmed my suspicions).

For a little while, we hiked through thick, thorny, vegetation until we finally found the first accessible point of the water. Drenched in sweat, I glanced up only to realize we had made it a mere 30 yards from where we started. We were both a bit unprepared. But we made the best of it. That's just what we do.

Equipped with waders, I wandered into the stream, trying to be as discreet as possible. I advanced far enough that Jordan had sufficient space to fish the waters behind me. Though it honestly didn't matter to either of us if the creek held any fish, there were more than a few around.

Once we settled in, the water in front of us began exploding. Every few minutes the noise of a jaw breaking the barrier of the water's surface made it clear the brook trout we desired were present. We were both excited. I had only caught one brookie in my life, by accident, when I was chasing bass and panfish with a slip bobber and nightcrawlers on the Mullet River in Plymouth. Jordan had never landed one.

Given my lack of experience with fly fishing and the self-taught nature of the little knowledge I possess on the subject, fly selection is not one of my strong suits. On this night, I was using my trusty black nymph. I viewed this bait as a fly fishing catch-all because, even though I don't fly fish often, this particular pattern has helped me land everything from smallmouth bass to carp. Sometimes, the best bait is the one you truly believe in.

Jordan utilized a caddis fly. We spent time catching up and shooting the bull as we went to work. No bites yet, but the fish were around.

Eventually, we decided to go back on land and begin casting from the bridge, with Jordan on the north side while I manned the south. Our luck turned slightly for the better. Jordan had a few fish break the surface in pursuit of his fly. I saw my line draw tight a few times, only to come up empty, just as he had. But it seemed we were onto something.

Darkness came and we were still empty-handed. But we learned a lot that evening. Not only was it clear that wading this stretch of water was probably ill-advised, but it was also apparent the fish preferred a surface presentation and that they generally hung out in the deeper portions of the creek.

My addiction got the better of me and I went back the next day with my wife, determined to capitalize on all the activity I had witnessed the previous night.

For a while, it was a carbon copy of the night before. A large brook trout greeted us with a splash when we were about 15 yards into the woods. Every once in a while, the serene sounds of the woodlands were disrupted by the echo of thrashing water as another fly fell victim to one of the apex predators below the surface. Despite all of this, I still hadn't managed a bite.

It was beginning to get dark, but I was able to catch a glimpse of my fly line quickly tightening. I grabbed the line with my right hand and pulled it downward and away from me. Finally, some resistance.

"This is it. This is my brook trout," I thought to myself. Lyza was at my side as I excitedly stripped line, bringing the fish closer to us. After a short back-and-forth, I brought the fish to us. Yes! There it was! But ... it wasn't a brook trout. To be honest,

I wasn't sure what it was. As best I could tell, it looked like an extremely large minnow. I took some pictures and released the fish. There was still just enough daylight left for a few more casts.

Moments later, the exact same scene played out. This time, though, I kept my guard up. Now that I knew there were hungry members of a non-target species in these waters my excitement was tempered.

It turned out I was right to take that approach. Whatever was attached to my fly certainly wasn't a brook trout. It was the same type of fish as before. I was puzzled but intrigued.

When we got home that night, I sent two of the pictures to a local fisheries biologist. I explained where I had caught the fish and asked him for some pointers in regard to identifying the fish.

I got a quick reply. "Looks like a creek chub, and it's a big one," he said.

If nothing else, being able to add a new species to my fishing log and more fish identification skills to my outdoors toolbox alleviated some of the frustration of not hooking into any of the numerous brookies we had seen over the past 48 hours.

I sent Jordan a couple of pictures of the chubs to jokingly prove to him that it was possible to actually catch fish in the spot I had explored with him. He responded with approval and a sense of renewed commitment to achieving our goal of landing a brook trout.

A couple of weeks later, we made new plans. We were eager to get out again and apply what we had learned on our previous trip toward scoring a brook trout.

Once again, we agreed to fish LaBudde Creek. But this time, we were going to fish a different portion of the property slightly north of where our last adventure took place. Jordan had waders this time. I'm sure his skin thanked him later.

We met at a rural parking lot near a stretch of the Ice Age Trail, a hiking trail that spans much of Wisconsin. Its roughly 1,200 miles wind from St. Croix Falls on the western border of the state to Sturgeon Bay in the east and are used by over 2.3 million people each year. Sheboygan County is home to a significant portion of this mileage, which runs through the Kettle Moraine State Forest.

After grabbing one of the crude maps provided at the entrance, we began our hike. Our scouting of this region was limited to satellite images we pulled up on our phones a few days before the trip. It was the dog days of summer and, even in the evening hours, the heat and humidity were impossible to ignore. Trudging along a hiking trail in insulated hunting waders didn't do anything to take our minds off those factors. But sometimes, catching a fish requires some literal legwork from the angler.

I often think of the first fishing trip to a new location to be a lot like the first pancake that goes in the pan. Every once in a while it may turn out alright and be somewhat enjoyable, but it will never be as satisfying as the ones that are to follow.

With that initial pancake, the issue is gauging the amount of heat in the pan. The first fishing trip similarly involves getting a feel for the new location and all of its variables.

While the quest for fishable waters was taking longer than I had anticipated, the landscape surrounding us was stunning. It had a little bit of everything, from hardwoods to gently rolling hills, grasslands to wetlands. If you would have blindfolded me and brought me to this place, I would have told you we were in Colorado. I couldn't believe all this was so close to where I live and I felt bad I hadn't spent any time here previously.

As our journey continued, I made note of potential deer hunting spots along our route (given the heat and humidity, I also noted how much it would absolutely suck to drag a deer out of most of these places). We then discussed the ins and outs of pheasant hunting and Jordan mentioned his desire to give that activity a try. I was able to get him out on a couple of pheasant hunts a few months later. But those are stories for another day.

We hiked all the way to the next county road without finding a spot where we could adequately access the creek. But the parcel of land across the road looked promising. We could see where the creek entered this chunk of land, so we followed it until we found a place we could cast.

Evening turning to dusk, we settled in on a small bend in the creek. Jordan entered the water and began casting toward some downed logs. I moved slightly downshore and found a suitable place to fish from the bank. It was close quarters, but it worked.

The water was crystal clear, appearing to be drinkable and refreshing, though it probably wasn't. Most bodies of water in this county don't appear that way.

I squinted as I tried to make out any fish-shaped objects before they set eyes on me. Fishing water with impeccable clarity is a give-and-take proposition. While it is easier to visually locate fish, it's also easier for the fish to see you.

The activity level of the fish here seemed to be significantly lower than it was to the south. There could have been a lot of factors at play, but there was no sense trying to sort through that. This was the spot we had with the time that remained. It was too late to change that.

In an amateur display, I got my line caught up on some brush and my leader snapped. Down a bait and another key piece of equipment, I had to problem-solve. I found some old strands of six-pound test line I had in my bag and fashioned an impromptu leader topped with a floating popper fly. Definitely not how a pro would do it, but it served the purpose. As disappointed as I was in my lack of preparation, I was equally proud of how I recovered and got back to fishing. A small part of me felt like Bear Grylls.

Daylight was rapidly diminishing and it became more difficult to see my bait skitter across the surface. I kept working methodically. Plop, pause, plop, pause, repeat. One of those plops was immediately followed by a burst shooting out of the water and it startled me, as the noise sang through the trees.

Unfortunately, that splash wasn't followed by any weight on the line. It was a clean miss.

I didn't want to leave now but Mother Nature wasn't going to give me much of a choice. A short time later, Jordan and I ventured out of the woods with the visibility that was provided by the day's final rays of sunshine. We walked the shoulders of a pair of county roads to get back to our parking spot, rambling about fishing and hunting along the way.

Nights like this always lower my blood pressure, even if the fish don't cooperate. I left that night grateful for a good friend and our ability to safely spend time together in the outdoors while challenging ourselves to improve at something new to us.

As of this writing, both of us have yet to catch a brook trout on a fly rod. But rest assured, we will continue trying and enjoying every minute of the process.

CHAPTER 8

Up North

Fish Nos. 45-49

"Up North" is a special place for so many people, both inside and outside of Wisconsin.

It's where Wisconsinites and tourists alike go to unplug, unwind and get away from the daily grind by partaking in activities like hiking, waterskiing, snowmobiling, riding ATVs, and of course, fishing.

If shopping and dining are more your speed, the Northwoods offers ample opportunity for that as well. There is an abundance of hole-in-the-wall foodservice operations and many of the larger cities have a host of shops downtown.

Downtown Eagle River is home to my favorite pizza joint, Alexander's, the type of shop where you order at the counter and dine at picnic tables. A plethora of arcade games line one side of the place. I've probably spent hours playing South Park pinball, Golden Tee Golf and Big Buck Hunter.

Back in the day, there was a store called All Things Jerky that offered dried and cured versions of nearly any meat you can think of, including alligator and ostrich.

The main drag is full of stores that range from full-on tourist traps selling airbrushed t-shirts to antique shops and a furniture store.

Each of the towns in this part of the world has its own combination of quirky small businesses. That's part of the reason why there is a little something for everyone in this small slice of heaven.

A longstanding debate continues to rage regarding which portions of our state constitute "up north." For some, it's anything on the high side of U.S. Highway 10. I fall into the camp of those who believe it begins once you cross U.S. Highway 8.

In an informal poll conducted by the Milwaukee Journal Sentinel several years ago, most respondents agreed with my assessment. That choice received more than half of the approximately 14,500 votes cast.

While I concede that one is certainly in the northern half of the state once crossing the Highway 10 threshold, I feel that you aren't truly up north until you are in a town where snowmobiles seem to outnumber cars in the wintertime—which, in this part of the state, can last from late October until mid-May.

In any case, as cheesy as it may sound, up north isn't so much a location as it is a state of mind and being. Life moves a little slower up north. I recall one evening sitting at the cabin and noting that the lead story on the local news broadcast was a feature on the new speed bumps that were recently installed in a nearby city.

Up north, the surroundings are relaxing and time is generally filled with healthy amounts of leisure.

A magnet on my parent's fridge reads, "The Northwoods are calling and I must go." Each summer, usually around the end of July, we answer that call. Our family spends a week in Vilas County on North and South Twin Lakes, a chain that spans over 3,500 acres. We've been doing this for more than a decade. Once in a while, a few spontaneous spring or fall trips helped us get our fix when necessary.

For most of the last two decades, we have rented a cabin in Conover from some family friends. The two-bedroom, one-bathroom abode overlooks North Twin and has everything we need to enjoy a comfortable stay: a fully-furnished kitchen, a dock with a boat lift, and a picnic table for enjoying the view.

As our family has grown, we have had to become more thoughtful about how we plan this trip. Though the cabin comfortably sleeps four, we have had to make alternative arrangements now that my sister and I have brought our spouses into the mix.

On occasion, we will rent out a neighboring cabin for one of the couples to stay at. Other times, we simply stagger our arrivals, with my sister Charlene and her husband Mitchell coming up at the beginning of the week and Lyza and I trekking up for the end. We do our best to make sure that we overlap for at least one afternoon so the six of us can enjoy some time together.

We generally split our time between fishing, eating, and exploring the local communities. This way, everyone in the family gets time for enjoying their favorite aspects of our surroundings.

When we're not on the water, we often spend time at many of the weekly flea markets in the nearby towns. My family's favorite is St. Germain. Each year, we spend time in the late morning and early afternoon browsing the aisles filled with dozens of vendors selling everything from wood carvings to fishing equipment.

As we have become more familiar with the area, my family has started to find a variety of local restaurants that became required stops on our vacation. We have fallen in love with the deep-dish pizza from the Log Cabin Inn, just down the road from the cabin. And we're suckers for any place that offers 50-cent chicken wings on a weeknight. Nearly every tavern in this area offers some sort of special during the week and most places let you dine right at the bar.

My mom tries to get ice cream at as many establishments as possible during our yearly excursion. On a few occasions, she has managed to track down an ice cream cone from a different shop each of the seven days of the trip.

But, for me, our trip up north is all about the fishing.

Noted for its muskie populations, the Twin Lakes chain is also home to world-class smallmouth bass fishing and plenty of walleye. It's a pristine fishery.

Though my wife and I weren't able to spend the full week with the family during this year's trip due to work obligations, I made it known that I wanted to spend more time focused on bass than we had in the past. Vilas County smallies dot numerous magazine covers throughout the year and are the subject of extensive conversation on forums and publications alike.

I wanted in. I wanted a fish worthy of a cover shot and I wanted to be sure we invested some time into this endeavor.

But my dad is a walleye junkie and he owns the boat, so our first voyage out was dedicated to the quest to add to the stock of fish in the freezer.

Shortly after Lyza and I arrived at the cabin, we got in the boat and headed to a bay on North Twin. My dad had found some success here earlier in the week while fishing with my mom, sister, and brother-in-law. We began trolling with spinning rods equipped with nightcrawler harnesses, a proven tactic that my dad often employed on his trips to Canada when I was younger.

Under these circumstances, bites feel more like little pulls or added weight rather than a pronounced strike or pop. This is because walleyes often grab the bait and hold it in their mouths rather than biting and thrashing like pike or bass would. Some people describe walleye biting a crawler harness as feeling like you snagged a wet bag.

On the Twin Lake chain, the scenery is almost as good as the fishing can be. Bald eagles soar and cackle; loons call and dive elegantly. Though there aren't as many as there used to be, a few remaining portions of the lake exhibit no signs of human life, the virgin forest untouched by even the smallest of cabins. The gap between the water's edge and the county road is filled with nothing more than trees and tall grass. Those are my favorite places on the lake to relax. After a couple of minutes, the true decompression starts. You can feel the stress leaving your body as the remarkably fresh air enters your lungs.

I was at the front of the boat, taking in all this goodness when my subconscious noticed my line felt a little heavier than it used to. There was something more than the natural water resistance against the egg sinker as the trolling motor putted along.

When I offered up a quick yank, the added weight remained. Fish on.

Walleyes are quite good at getting heavy. They use force to their advantage when they find themselves on the end of a line.

The fish did its best to resist but eventually found its way into the landing net. It was a hair over 15 inches, just long enough to keep per the lake's regulations. We dropped it in the live well and continued fishing. At least we weren't going home empty-handed.

After another hour or so, and nothing to show for it, we called it quits. Only one fish to our credit, but it was good to be back.

Later that day, after lunch and a bit of shopping in nearby Eagle River, we got in the boat with the idea of targeting bass. The wind was blowing fiercely from the north. This made boat control difficult, but we fished through it. As we systematically went from spot to spot, I tossed about every type of bass lure I had. Plastics, spinners, spoons, crankbaits, swim baits — I threw the tacklebox at them and had nothing to show for it. Neither did my dad or Lyza.

We moved to our last spot for the afternoon, near the boat launch. The gentle curve of the shoreline was just pronounced enough to offer some respite from the enduring wind.

I alternated between my three rods, each with a different style of bait attached. My dad had a couple of bites on his Senko, but the skunk was still present in our boat.

Then, out of the corner of my eye, I saw Lyza reeling vigorously. She had made a connection and was now imploring the fish to move toward the boat. "Come on," she said while applying pressure to the pole, trying to gain the upper hand in this exchange. "Get over here."

Her lure was a green and silver Little Cleo spoon, meaning the fish on the receiving end could be just about anything that inhabits these waters.

We caught a glimpse of the fish, a briefly visible flash of golden hue. Given its shape, this was probably a bass. She muscled the fish into the net. It was a nice smallmouth, but not the kind we came here for. Still, we were onto something and our afternoon on the water wasn't in vain. Not that time on the water ever truly is.

The following morning, we were back out for walleye. My mom joined the three of us, adding another ticket for the fish lottery.

I was in my usual spot at the front of the boat when I scored another keeper walleye. More time passed, but no other fish joined our crew. We decided to switch our focus to bass before we headed back in.

We ventured away from our drop-off and toward the nearby shoreline and began tossing. Lyza was working her Little Cleo. I opted for the stick bait and my dad was again using his trusty old Senko. My mom sat in the passenger seat, enjoying the scenery and participating in our wide-ranging conversations that took place over the country radio playing in the background courtesy of Coyote Country 93.7 FM in Eagle River.

Music on the boat is something of a hot topic among anglers I've encountered. Some swear that playing the radio scares fish. Others have superstitions related to the type of music they listen to on the water. Our family friend Lee swears the muskies on North Twin love polka. It's really just a matter of personal preferences and belief systems.

"There's one," my dad called out mid-hookset. Immediately, it became clear that this wasn't going to be a garden-variety encounter with a swimming creature. The drag screamed as the rod bent in half. My dad stood up from his casting stool, putting his entire body into the fight.

Lyza grabbed the net and joined my dad at the front of the boat. I never saw the fish while it was in the water, but the reaction that came from my wife and father upon seeing the fish for the first time told me all I needed to know.

"Whoa!" shouted Lyza.

"This is a big one," my dad chimed in with a bit of anxiety in his voice.

"Don't horse it. Don't horse it," I called out to my dad with shades of concern and anxiety. Losing this fish would sting.

Moments later, Lyza lunged over the side of the boat with the net. What followed was a string of excited expletives from everyone on board except my mom. She was excited but maintained her composure a little better than the three of us. I caught the entire exchange on video.

My dad reached into the net and produced what was, at that point in my life, the largest smallmouth bass I had ever seen in person. It was my old man who had scored the fish worthy of a magazine cover.

I rifled through the glove compartment in search of a measuring device. Eventually, I produced a rusty silver tape measure. We quickly took as many measurements as we could. This fish would be going on the wall (well, kind of). My dad, still shaking from the thrill of it all, managed to open his phone and record the dimensions I read off to him.

The fish was a touch under 18 inches in length and more than 7 inches in width. A true football.

My dad released the fish and we traded high-fives. Even though I wasn't an active player, the whole thing was incredibly exciting.

The boat ride home, and much of the remaining day, was spent discussing the merits of getting a replica made. After the flurry of excitement that comes with catching a personal-best fish, the adrenaline eventually begins to wear off and you start to think more clearly. That's when anglers often start to second-guess themselves about committing to the investment of getting a mount or replica produced. While the definition of a "trophy" is in the eye of the beholder, it is natural to anticipate the judgment that will come from others who view the specimen hanging on the wall. This is where many people ask themselves, "Is this fish truly as impressive as I think it is?"

By the end of the day, my dad decided the answer to that question was "yes" and had decided to move forward with this process. His replica now hangs in a place of honor among the rest of his mounts above the landing leading to the upstairs of my parents' house.

That afternoon, it was time for our annual panfish outing. We make a point of spending at least a little time chasing bluegills, sunfish, and perch each year because they provide fast-paced action and account for most of the fish we keep for eating. So we will dedicate at least an afternoon or two putting in the time to make that happen.

In our best years, we'd score over 1,000 panfish in a week between myself, my mom, my dad, and my sister. It doesn't require much patience or skill – just a certain level of knowledge of the habitat and depths you are looking for, paired with spinning rods set up with slip bobbers and a steady supply of nightcrawlers. In the past, most of these fish were found on South Twin. But the lake has been dealing with invasive Eurasian Milfoil in recent years and its presence has really put a damper on the panfish bite.

This year, we chose to give North Twin a shot. The owner of the cabin we stayed at and his son-in-law had been kind enough to offer up a few spots the night prior.

I'm always appreciative when I receive tidbits like this. Even on a body of water the size of the Twin Lakes chain, many of the locals are protective of their spots and the resources their home lakes have to offer.

This place is like a second home to them and many of these folks take great care when considering how many and which fish to keep. Being willing to share intel on hot spots is a sign of trust and I do my best to prove worthy of that through the decisions I make about harvesting fish and passing this information on to others.

Even with this new knowledge, I was still in bass mode, especially after what I witnessed in the hours before. I wanted a fish like my dad's. So I stuck to my smallmouth gear while the other three plopped their bobbers out. The trio managed just under a dozen fish in a fairly short timespan. It wasn't steady enough, but the beauty of this chain is that, if you don't find a lot of panfish quickly, you can rest assured you are better served picking up and moving to another one of its numerous hotspots.

We headed south, stopping behind an island just before the channel where the pair of lakes meet. It was substantially deeper than the previous spot, but the habitat looked better. Despite the depth, a variety of aquatic plants were visible as they grew upward, reaching toward the nourishing sunlight.

Being stubborn, I continued to stand in the back of the boat casting for smallies. Meanwhile, the action rapidly became hot and heavy for the other three members of the crew. The pace of bites was much closer to what they had been accustomed to.

Eventually, I broke down and joined them, but in my own way. I chose a hair jig tipped with the slightest bit of worm and slowly guided the bait over the tops of the weeds. This produced some very solid rock bass and I was pleased with the results.

We ended the trip with 75 fish. I contributed a whopping three.

I fished the dock at the cabin after sunset that night, with only a handful of bites to show for my efforts. It gave me an excuse to use our collection of light-up bobbers, one of the coolest fishing gadgets ever invented, in my opinion.

The next morning brought with it the final hours of our trip. We made one last trek to our familiar bay in search of walleye and bass, but came up empty.

Then it was time to pack and load up the boat. Once the final chores were done, Lyza and I hopped in the truck and pointed it south.

We spent the ride home discussing options for how we could answer the call of the Northwoods a little more often.

I dreamed about the possibility of Lyza and I someday owning our own cabin on the lake and being able to fish whenever I wanted. We talked about a future life when our time could be split between being out on the water, rummaging through local flea markets, and eating at our favorite dive bars.

It will be a good while before any of that could possibly be a reality, but I find peace knowing that, no matter what, I will be answering the call of the Northwoods, one way or another, before too long.

CHAPTER 9

Tough Lessons

Fish Nos. 80-82

When I'm out on the water and the action is a little slow, my mind can easily wander off.

As I lose myself in the serenity of the breeze gently kissing the water or the warmth of the sun on my skin, I often end up pondering how I fit into the grand scheme of things. What is my place in the give-and-take arena of the natural world? Am I holding up my end of the bargain?

Conservation has become a growing part of my thought process when out fishing. This transition had to happen because the more fish one comes into contact with, the larger the potential impact on the environment becomes. These days, I am hooking into more fish than I would in a typical year.

Each day, fish will die and it has to be that way. It's just part of the order of the natural world and we, as humans, are a part of that order.

The key is attempting to have a minimal influence on that cycle by safely releasing fish I do not intend to keep. After all, fish are a finite resource. But they play a crucial role in their ecosystems.

Fish can store and transport nutrients in their tissues. When they excrete those nutrients, they provide a forage base for vital microorganisms that lay the framework for the food chain.

Our finned companions also serve as a food source for creatures above them on that chain, including a variety of birds, humans, and other fish. Mismanagement of a fish population can throw the entire cycle out of whack.

The quality of fisheries management in most of the places where I spend my time depends on more than just my actions, but I like to focus on what I can control and do my best to be a steward of the outdoors.

From my point of view, it is almost always easier to protect what you already have than to attempt to reintroduce a species that used to be present in a given location. Conserving is generally preferable to rehabilitation.

So I started to become more intentional about how I handled and released the fish I was catching. Rather than gently tossing small fish back, I began lowering them into the water and letting them swim away as I gave up my grasp, just as I would with a larger specimen that could be jarred by colliding with the surface of the water when haphazardly tossed back.

This is why I also make sure to support fish with two hands any time I hold them horizontally to avoid applying unnecessary stress to their jaws and spines.

These may seem like small things, but doing them consistently made me feel like I was doing my part to help promote healthy fisheries. A variety of studies conducted in different states in recent years suggests the survival rate of a properly-released fish is somewhere between 84 and 98 percent. The better (and faster) the release, the better the odds.

Maybe this makes me overly optimistic, but I have a working theory that most anglers truly care about the fish they pursue.

I'd like to believe few people go fishing feeling indifferent about whether or not they harm the fish they catch. And I am certainly not among those few. Through my journaling I've found that, In a typical year, I release over 98 percent of the fish I catch.

My Grandpa Tony and my dad grew up in a fishing culture where most anglers didn't think twice about keeping fish. After all, being able to enjoy a fish dinner after a successful outing was a big part of the fun. There was a sense of pride in saying you came home with your limit of a particular species.

Throughout the years, I've found that my approach differs from that of my elder family members who seemed more focused on keeping fish to eat. I view fish as a resource to be enjoyed by as many people as possible. Releasing fish helps make that vision a reality.

Besides, the low water quality of many of the locations I frequent makes some fish less than a desirable meal.

There isn't anything wrong with keeping a few fish for the table and I am more than willing to do that on occasion. But I try to be mindful of my impact on any fishery I come into contact with by being selective about the size and number of fish I keep.

It was mid-August when I made the 20-minute drive west of my hometown to pursue northern pike at the Glenbeulah Millpond, a spot I primarily fish in winter when I want to chase tip-ups and enjoy a few beers with my friends.

The pike in this spot are almost always small, but they are abundant. This is an action spot. During ice fishing season, it's nothing to catch over two dozen northerns in a morning, though nearly all of them will be under 16 inches. There was one notable exception to this.

On one bitterly cold morning in mid-December of 2013, my friend Cody pulled up a 33-inch pike on a tip-up. We celebrated like we had won the lottery. In a way, we kind of did. In nearly a decade of fishing in this location since that day, my friends and I haven't caught anything near that size here. That particular memory always seems to make its way into the front of my mind whenever I'm in Glenbeulah, whether I'm fishing or not.

As I came back to the reality of the late-summer of 2020, I departed the world of wind chills and found myself once again in the midst of an 80-degree late-summer evening.

Up until this point in the season, I had been able to successfully release nearly all of the fish that I didn't intend to keep. I take pride in honing the craft of safe fish releases. In recent years, my definition of a "good release" has evolved.

On this night, I walked to my spot carrying my black fishing backpack, a spinning rod, and a baitcasting rod with my secret weapon tied to the end of the line: an orange and silver ⅖-ounce Little Cleo spoon. This bait has been quite good to me over the years, but it is especially effective when fishing for pike.

Even though fall was lurking in the not-so-distant future, it was very much a summer evening. The sun was shining, with temperatures in the low 80s and negligible wind. Not exactly pike weather, which is generally on the cooler side, but I was still optimistic.

At the millpond, it generally doesn't take long to figure out what kind of a trip you're about to have, especially if you are using the right bait.

Pike are aggressive, opportunistic feeders that will quickly make their presence known if you are doing things correctly. And this spot is full of hungry (albeit small) pike.

I made the short walk from the parking area, crossing a

narrow metal bridge over a dam to my first spot that sits right next to the beginning of a hiking path at the entrance of a woods.

Most of the shoreline is dotted with piles of white rocks, bleached by the sun, that are likely meant to protect the soil on shore against erosion during high-water times of year. The depth of the pond is fairly consistent throughout, rarely exceeding five feet.

First, I fastened a nightcrawler to the single hook that was affixed to the end of the line on the spinning rod, just below a pair of split shot sinkers. I planned to use this rod as a feeler setup for bass. While I had never caught a bass here, I've been told they are present and that some are quite large.

With the bait in the water floating just above the bottom, I rested my rod on my tackle box and reeled in slowly until the line was taut. Any movement from the rod tip would alert me to a bite.

Next, I grabbed the baitcaster and began to cover water with the Little Cleo. I positioned my casts in a fan pattern, hoping to maximize the area I was fishing until I could dial in a more specific location that held hungry fish.

To my surprise, the spinning rod was the first to get a strike. I dropped my baitcaster mid-retrieval and ran to my left, grabbing the spinning rod. I set the hook and felt a quick connection. There was a fair amount of pressure on the line and my heart began racing as my mind entertained thoughts of the sizable bass that could be on the other end. After all, there was a worm on this hook and I can count on one hand the number of times I've hooked into a northern while using a nightcrawler.

The fish remained hidden below the surface of the water as the fight played out. Eventually, I muscled the fish closer to shore. As it entered the shallows, my adversary became visible. This wasn't a bass. In fact, it was a white sucker, a bottom-feeding fish that is technically a member of the minnow family.

I brought the fish ashore, unhooked it, snapped a few pictures and sent the fish back on its way. It's always nice to get a fish early, even if it wasn't one you were expecting to find.

After equipping the hook with a fresh worm, I reset the rod and turned my attention back to the baitcaster. It didn't take long to score a bite.

The lure was about 20 yards from shore when I felt a pair of taps on the end of the line, followed by a lack of pressure. The fish was swimming toward me and I had to quickly reel in the newly created slack to maintain a stable connection with the fish. After a few feverish cranks, I was able to catch up to the fish and began to feel its full power.

Though it was a small specimen, it was full of vigor and darting about now that it realized its predicament.

In short order, the fish was on shore with all three of the treble hooks at the bottom of the lure securely in its mouth. This fish certainly qualified as a "hammer handle," a slang term that is assigned to small pike due to their shape and length.

I grabbed my yellow-handled needle-nose pliers and freed the fish from the trio of hooks. I walked it back to the water line, lowering it to the surface. When I felt the fish begin to swim, I released my gentle grip and the pike swam off back toward where it came from.

After that, action became hard to come by. I began methodically working my way toward the truck as the evening turned to night, pausing on occasion to focus on pockets of unfished water.

It was just after sunset when I arrived at my final spot, a shallow weed bed that was accessible from a location mere yards from the parking area. This location can be tricky. While it certainly holds fish, the thick vegetation makes bait presentation challenging. You have to work the lure fast enough to keep it out of the weeds, but not so fast that it begins cruising on the surface at a rate that is too rapid for a reluctant pike to give chase.

On my very first cast, I felt a pull followed by added weight on the end of the line. I hadn't even started reeling yet. I must have hit this fish right on the head.

When I set the hook, I was greeted with a big splash about 30 yards from my spot on the shoreline. This was no hammer handle.

The fish made a run to my left and, in the process, tried to make itself as heavy as possible. I kept steady tension on the line, trying to eliminate the fish's chance to gain leverage while also attempting to not apply so much pressure that I would pull the lure out of its mouth.

It took a few minutes, but I eventually got the fish to shore. It wasn't a monster by traditional standards but, at over two feet long, it was one of the larger pike I had come across in my 10-plus years fishing this spot.

There was a problem, though. The fish had swallowed nearly all of the lure. The silver split ring at the top of the spoon was the only portion of the bait that was visible.

With even the faintest sense of remaining daylight in short supply, I grabbed my pliers and tried to quickly get to work. I couldn't get the hooks to budge. After what felt like an eternity, I grabbed the fish and held it in the water, trying to allow it to catch its breath without lodging the hooks even deeper in its mouth.

After a couple of minutes, I tried again to free the hooks. Still, to no avail. A jaw spreader would have been a huge help here.

But I didn't have one. A headlamp would have made life easier too, but I didn't have one of those either. I was basically doing this blind.

Eventually, through nothing other than stupid luck, I was able to remove the hooks. I rushed the fish to the water, held it in place for a while and then let it go. The release didn't feel good. While the fish swam off on its own accord, it didn't do so with the usual vigor of an apex predator that was placed back into its domain. Rather than taking off out of my hand with purpose, it lethargically wandered back toward deeper waters.

A few minutes later, the fish emerged on the surface. It was dead. And it was because of my lack of preparation. I felt terrible.

While there is nothing wrong with keeping fish, killing a fish you don't intend to keep is a different story.

Then it occurred to me: if I could land the fish again, at least I could take it home and eat it. Stupidly, I didn't have my net on me. So I ran back to the truck to retrieve it.

In that time, the fish had drifted too far away from shore to be scooped with my meager landing net.

I spent a few minutes sitting at the edge of the dark pond out of breath and feeling defeated.

The ride home was spent in silence, beating myself up for my numerous miscues. I took some solace in the fact that nature doesn't waste. Some bird of prey or even another pike would likely make a meal of this fish that it would not have otherwise had.

If nothing else, the microorganisms in the water would have something to feed on. Still, I struggled to get over the level of my stupidity. This situation was largely avoidable. But I was unprepared.

No matter how well-intentioned we are, bad things can

happen any time we encounter wild creatures. The more fish you come across, the more opportunity you have to injure or even kill a fish you planned on releasing. It's part of life. Even the best anglers can't control everything. The key is to be as prepared as possible for a host of situations and to do what you can to control the things you have influence on.

As cheesy as it may sound, I'm a big believer in learning from your mistakes. When I got home, I went online and ordered a jaw spreader. It has accompanied me on every single fishing trip I have taken since that night.

I used to just be focused on getting the fish back into the water quickly. But I have come to learn that giving the fish the best chance to live involves so much more than that.

Holding the fish properly by supporting its weight correctly when it is out of the water is a crucial component of the release process. Having a landing net and the proper tools for dislodging finicky hooks is another.

The fact is: you just never know when you will have to deal with a deeply-hooked fish. Time is critical in these situations and having a plan is critical.

A few weeks later, I returned to Glenbeulah with my brother-in-law Mitchell. Toward the end of the night, we shot a video that I posted to YouTube entitled "Must-have pike fishing gear for beginners." That video prominently featured a landing net and a jaw spreader to go along with a pair of pliers.

I wanted to do my part to prevent others from having to go through the unfortunate experience that I endured on this day.

Though I didn't know it at the time, that video became the kickstarter for my outdoors brand: Nathan Woelfel Outdoors (more on that later).

For now, I found solace in the fact that I had grown as an angler and wasn't likely to repeat these mistakes again.

CHAPTER 10

The Big One

Fish. No. 120

Anticipation is one of the best parts of any fishing excursion. At any point, you could be moments away from the fish of a lifetime. This was exactly the experience that awaited me on a gloomy Sunday afternoon in early September.

I decided to sneak off to a nearby spot on the Sheboygan River, Settlers Park, for a relaxing session. This modest, two-acre park came to be in 2001 when I was 10 years old. It features little more than a few trees, a couple of picnic tables, and a gazebo that is used for weddings and the occasional summer concert.

It was a familiar place. As a child, I spent many a hot day wading around these stained waters that are filled with silt and mud, catching dozens of undersized, yet feisty, smallmouth bass along with the occasional carp or bullhead.

My Grandpa Wally and Grandma Ruth lived just a couple blocks away and would often come to visit my friends and me on hot summer afternoons to chat and see how the fishing was.

Sometimes grandma would bring a couple of bags of Cheetos or potato chips for us to snack on during our rare breaks from fishing.

When I was in middle school, my sister and I would walk home to my grandparents' house after school. If my homework was completed, I occasionally ventured off for a quick trip to the dam for some fishing before my parents got done with work and came to take us home.

Every once in a while, when I'm fishing at Settlers Park, I drift back to those days and fondly recall the simpleness of childhood and the warm feelings that came from my grandparents' steady presence in it.

I've come to view this as a numbers spot. You will almost always catch plenty of fish, primarily smallmouth with the occasional panfish or bullhead mixed in. But most of them are nothing to write home about.

One time, I was taken by surprise as I pulled up a rainbow trout from a pocket of water near the dam. It was likely a survivor of our city's "Free Fishing Day."

Each year, on the first weekend of June, Wisconsin anglers can fish without a license. The event is meant to generate fresh interest in outdoor activities. The DNR stocks the lagoon in River Park with roughly 1,000 rainbow trout for new anglers to target. Given there is a dam separating this spot from Lake Michigan, the primary home of rainbows in our area, this fish was most likely from the planting that occurred earlier in the year.

During the springtime, pre- and post-spawn bass over the 14-inch mark become a bit more prevalent. In summer or early fall, any bass over 12 inches is unlikely to come from this segment of the river.

But that doesn't keep me from visiting this spot on occasion.

I will almost never turn down the opportunity for consistent action, especially when I'm pinched for time.

On this day, I opted to fish from shore rather than wade into the silty water. Wading requires thoughtful packing because it forces you to carry only what you need (and what you can keep dry). This was a spur-of-the-moment trip and I didn't want to invest the necessary time into that sort of preparation.

I set off with a pair of spinning rods and a container of nightcrawlers from the gas station down the road. I selected one of my go-to setups, a single hook with half a worm accompanied by a pair of split shot sinkers a few inches above the hook's eye. The bait sits just off the bottom and when the rod tip begins bouncing, the action begins.

It became clear the fish were holed up just outside of the main current in a seam between the slack water and the faster-moving stuff. In short order, I flipped a half-dozen smallies ashore before they were promptly returned to their world.

My two rods were spaced out along the fence that lines roughly half the property from the dam to about the midway point of the paved walking path that weaves through the park. The black metal fence is briefly interrupted by the presence of a wood patio that overlooks the river. A wooden railing that stands about waist-high ensures secure viewing for visitors and a place for anglers to rest their fishing poles.

Most of the time, the fence was only a minor obstacle to landing fish, particularly the smaller ones. With a quick pull of the line, it was easy to guide the fish over the railing, unhook it, and walk it to a spot closer to water level for release.

While I knew where the active fish were, I didn't want to put all my eggs in one basket. When it came down to it, there were only going to be so many fish feeding in the initial spot and I wanted to have a sense of where my next move could be.

The next strike wasn't anything out of the ordinary. The rod tip danced vigorously, indicating life on the other end of the line. I jogged over, reeled up my slack, and set the hook. Instantly, I knew something was different about the intensity of this battle.

There was a weight there that strayed greatly from the fish I had caught earlier that day. "This has to be a carp," I said out loud to my audience of one. While those sizable bottom feeders were not prevalent in this stretch of the river, they are plentiful in the Sheboygan River as a whole. Encountering one just below the Sheboygan's second dam is not unheard of and it is something I have experienced on a handful of occasions. In fact, my dad had landed a small carp in this spot while on a trip with me just a few weeks prior.

The fish fought its way against the current, taking drag as it moved from right to left toward the dam. I had a bird's-eye view of the action from my position about 12 feet above the water's surface. Perhaps the fish was in search of deeper waters, or maybe it was simply enjoying the leverage that came from the added tension on the line. Either way, about a minute into the fight, the fish still had not shown itself to me.

Doing my best to remain patient, I adjusted the drag settings on my reel and kept my rod tip high. As best I could tell, it seemed like this fish was hooked pretty well.

Eventually, the skirmish reversed course and headed downriver several yards to my right. With the current now to my advantage, I quickly made headway and drew the fish closer, still not knowing exactly what I was dealing with.

With the fish out of the current and heading toward the slack water about 15 yards from me, I caught my first glimpse. It had the body shape of a larger specimen, but the color was not indicative of a carp. With only so many species inhabiting this portion of the river, the bronze tones visible through the water's reflection told me this was a bass. A big one.

My blood pressure began to trend upward thanks to a nice spike in adrenaline. The stakes were so much higher now. I've caught (and lost) plenty of carp in my life. But a bass the size this one appeared to be? I had never tangled with one personally, much less landed one.

The fish began to tire, but the fight was far from over. It darted back into the seam, trying to recapture the upper hand it held when the battle began in the current produced by the water being forced over the dam. But with my adversary lacking the spunk it had at the onset, I was able to head it off and keep the fish toward my side of the faster water and direct it to the shoreline.

But I had another problem. Even though the fish was near the shore, it was 10 feet below the edge of the patio where I stood. A net would never reach. Walking it downshore to a place I could access the river at water level was a risky proposition that involved a 30-yard stroll while navigating around the trees and bushes that lined the river's edge, all the while maintaining enough tension on the line to prevent the battle from extending to another round.

Flipping it over the fence, as I did with the other fish, also came with its fair share of drawbacks, the most pressing of which was the high probability of the line breaking under the intense pressure of the fish's size, coupled with the height differential between our current positions.

It was not an ideal plan, but attempting to flip the fish seemed like the best option I had. In an attempt to mitigate risk, I shuffled to my right into a patch of shrubs. This placed me about two feet closer to the water than I previously was. I eliminated the slack, held my breath, and yanked.

The fish began its rapid ascent to land. Though it happened in a matter of seconds, the fish's trip from the water to the shore seemed to take minutes. It felt like everything was happening in slow motion.

While the fish was in mid-flight, a loud snap rang out. The line gave way. But the fish had made it over the railing and was thrashing in the brush behind me; momentum had taken the fish over my right shoulder and into the mulch that lined the landscaping. The fish was desperately trying to make its way to the fence and back to the water. I pounced on it like a linebacker after a fumble. The monster was secured between my chest and chin. By the slimmest of margins, the gamble paid off.

Quickly, I grabbed the fish by the mouth and ran back to my tackle box. Sand was slipping through the hourglass and time wasn't on my side if I wanted to safely release this trophy. I rummaged through the chaos that is my bottom compartment and found my measuring tape. After a few quick measurements, I snapped a handful of pictures while I began formulating a release plan. Smallmouth bass this size are unheard of in most of this river. This made a safe release even more critical.

Given the relative altitude of my spot, releasing the fish from my perch on the weathered patio was not in the cards. I briskly walked down the shoreline to a spot that granted me direct access to the water. I gently placed the fish back, holding its tail while it regained its bearings. After a few moments, my hands could feel the fish's increasing levels of resistance. I released my grasp and the fish slowly cruised back into the middle of the river, not far from where I found it—hopefully to eventually reproduce or perhaps to even be caught again by another fortunate angler who will someday have a story like mine.

In a river like this, with a finite amount of food and suitable habitat, it can take north of eight years to grow a smallmouth of this stature. I don't take facts like that for granted when I consider how I go about the catch-and-release process.

It never occurred to me to keep the fish. I certainly wanted to preserve the memory. But keeping a fish from this treasured spot just so I could have another decoration on my wall seemed a little selfish to me. I am confident I took all the measurements and pictures necessary to get a replica made and I think that is an avenue I am going to take in the near future, if I can justify the financial investment and feel confident I have a prominent place on my wall to feature it.

With a length of 19 inches and a weight of just over 3 pounds, this tank of a fish was by far the largest bass I had caught in my life. It was slightly longer than the skinny 33-ounce bottle of electrolyte water I had with me with the goal of staying hydrated during my outing. My focus was gone. I fired off a flurry of text messages and pictures to my family and fishing buddies. My parents, who were out and about running errands even stopped at the park to hear my newest tale firsthand.

I was simultaneously overjoyed and in complete disbelief.

The unlikely location of the catch made it even more special. In my lifetime, I have been fortunate enough to pull hundreds of smallies from this chunk of river. And I had never caught anything that would even remotely suggest that a fish this large could be cruising around. It was a gift from my hometown and a childhood hotspot that I will forever treasure.

CHAPTER 11

Exploring My Competitive Side

Fish Nos. 142-177

Most of us have a competitive streak. It may not be apparent on the surface, but eventually, it will be brought to light, whether it is through sports, our work lives, or playing board games with our family and friends.

Save for a handful of salmon derbies I fished with my dad and grandpa in my teenage years, I had never really given much thought to applying my competitiveness toward anything related to the outdoors.

In late August, I saw a Facebook ad for an online bass tournament through a company called Lucky Go Fishing. Though I wasn't familiar with the organization, a little research on Facebook and Google led me to the conclusion that it was legitimate. After chewing on the thought of competing for a few days, I decided to see what I was made of and submitted my entry.

At this point in the year, I was beginning to realize that I was kind of good at this "fishing" thing. While I wasn't about to turn pro, the previous months had taught me that, at the very least, my fishing acumen was above average.

The tournament was slated for the last weekend of September. I began scoping out spots and trying new tactics almost immediately. This time, I viewed my outings through the lens of a tournament angler.

It was the first week of September when Lucky Go Fishing sent an email regarding a one-day members-only tournament coming up the following weekend. They were short on people to make the whole thing work from a financial standpoint. To bolster the field, they were opening up some slots for non-members who might be interested.

I took them up on their offer, even though most of my fellow competitors would be fishing in boats, a luxury I didn't have. The tournament was less than a week away, but I felt ready.

The field was divided into geographic regions. Entrants from across the country were allowed to fish any waters within their region on that particular Saturday. Contestants had to photograph their fish while on a trough-style measuring device with a personalized identification code included (to ensure the fish were caught the day-of) and submitted via a mobile app. The five longest fish counted toward your total. The angler with the highest total in each of the three regions wins. The top three places in each region paid out. Largemouth or smallmouth bass were acceptable. Spotted bass, where applicable, were also fair game.

Even though most of the competitors were, presumably, utilizing boats, I was confident that, given adequate fishing time and preparation, I could hold my own. As fall approached, local rivers continued to shallow out. This concentrated many of the fish in relatively deeper pockets that remained. The fish became considerably more active as they began to pack on pounds with the approach of winter. The memory of catching the largest bass of my life in one of these spots just a couple of weeks prior was fresh in my mind and it certainly bolstered my confidence.

There was one concern that wouldn't leave my mind: the weather. Rain was in the forecast for both the overnight and morning hours. Too much precipitation in a short period of time could render many of my best spots unfishable either due to current or lack of visibility for the fish.

The night before the tournament was spent getting my mind and my gear in order. Rods appropriately rigged, tackle box organized, backpack packed. My list of hot spots received an update based on my latest experiences and I was confident in my plan.

Then, as advertised, the rain came. It wasn't hard, but it was steady enough to be heard pattering against the back window in the kitchen as I locked the back door before heading to bed. I went from being full of optimism to increasingly concerned that I might not catch a fish at all.

Nerves and excitement kept me from getting meaningful sleep. Much of the night was spent restlessly rolling back and forth, trying not to disturb Lyza as I tried to steal a glimpse at the alarm clock. I was determined to make the best of my first tournament, no matter what Mother Nature planned to throw my way.

My alarm wasn't required because I was wide awake before it even went off. Grabbing my phone and opening the tournament app, I jotted down my identifier on the back of a piece of cardboard I ripped off the Busch Light case that was sitting at the bottom of my basement staircase. The thought was that cardboard had a better chance of maintaining its integrity during the damp weather than a piece of paper would.

There were 30 anglers in my region, spanning much of the Midwest, including Illinois, Michigan, and Minnesota.

It was about a half-hour before dawn as I packed up my gray 2018 Ford F-150. I love my truck because it is the vehicle I have always wanted. It's the nicest truck I've ever owned, especially when compared to the tan Ford Ranger I drove in high school and the beat-up old two-door work truck I bought shortly after Lyza and I got married.

In its former life, my F-150 was a company vehicle for a Ford employee who decided to trade it in for the next year's model after less than a year of use. This made it the best truck I could afford for the price.

Its four-door cab is spacious and comfortable, while the bed is big enough to haul all of my fishing gear. My truck accompanies me on nearly every fishing trip and I am so thankful I have it.

The plan was to head to Settlers Park. I wanted to start at a place where I could reasonably expect to catch a high volume of fish. Few things are more embarrassing than the thought of entering a tournament only to not register a single fish.

A light rain persisted but, surprisingly, the overnight showers had not negatively impacted the water levels in a noticeable way.

I got some music flowing through my headphones, a little Metallica to get my blood pumping and elevate my energy level, as my first two lines hit the water. Using any means necessary to keep my energy level up and spirits high throughout the day would be imperative. On lengthy solo fishing trips, I often turn to music to accomplish that task. My wide-ranging playlists are heavy on music from the late 90s and early 2000s, a steady diet of the music I grew up on, everything from Alan Jackson to the Backstreet Boys. You can even find most of Britney Spears' Greatest Hits album sprinkled throughout my music library.

My initial approach was to deadstick with nightcrawlers, the same method that yielded my personal-best bass. It didn't take long for my anxiety to ease. Fish No. 1 of the day came in short order. An 8-inch smallmouth. I recorded the catch in the app and breathed a sigh of relief.

A rush of excitement and anticipation came over me. The prospect of every fish, even if it wasn't big, just felt like it meant more. It's an awesome feeling of pure adrenaline that isn't often experienced on my average fishing trips.

From there, the catches became more frequent, even as the rain picked up. But the issue quickly became their lack of size. My biggest bass was only 9.5 inches—hardly what I needed to put up a competitive effort. With five scorable fish already to my credit, I needed to bump up my average length.

Around 9:30 a.m., I decided to pick up and move on to spot No. 2 on the list: the Flats. This stretch of the Sheboygan River definitely held fewer fish than the previous location, but the average size is usually a nice step up from what I found in the early going.

The rain became steadier. I was already on my second jacket. My first water-resistant outer shell had already succumbed to the persistent precipitation and the layer underneath was becoming heavy as uncomfortable dampness set in.

One of the first fish I pulled out of the new spot was 10.5 inches. I at least had a double-digit bass to my credit. A short time later, a 12.25-incher came over the rail. This was the size of the fish I came here for. I started feeling better about my day, even if the weather wasn't looking up.

Once I felt I had caught all of the active fish I was going to catch at the Flats, I moved downriver to Rochester Park. I caught a 13-inch smallie there during my pre-fishing and a fish that size would do wonders for my average.

I found about a half-dozen more fish, but nothing of the size I hoped. I decided to move back to my original spot, optimistic things had picked back up. Lyza was kind enough to drop off some lunch. She asked about my morning and offered some words of encouragement before getting me up to speed on her grocery shopping trip and happenings around the house.

Quickly snacking on a sandwich, a "Pepe" from Jimmy John's, I went back to fishing. Things hadn't picked up. I caught another 10-incher, but nothing else to write home about. This was a dead end.

Early afternoon was turning to mid-afternoon as I ventured west briefly to River Park. The lagoon there showed some promise in the lead-up to the tournament. I had missed a relatively good-sized smallie there just 48 hours earlier on a chartreuse spinnerbait. I snapped that very bait onto my swivel and went back to the place I last saw the fish. Nothing.

I worked the bank to both the left and right of my starting point. More casts, but still no fish. It was at this point I opted for a new spot: Anton Park in Plymouth on the Mullet River. I pulled some good smallies out of there in the summertime. Admittedly though, I hadn't done my homework on this location in the week before the tournament and I paid dearly for that.

When I arrived, I tried spinners, Rapalas, and live bait. I couldn't buy a hit and I was running out of time.

It was around 3:30 p.m. when I arrived at Woodlake, the next spot on my list. The Kohler hotspot was a bit of a longshot, but there was no doubt it held fish in the size range I needed to improve my place in the standings.

With the rain continuing to fall, I walked down the gravel path to my first spot. Honestly, I had become so accustomed to the incessant precipitation that I hardly noticed it at this point. When I arrived at my initial spot, I found that all of the weed beds were gone. Dead. This cover is critical to holding bass near shore. Without it, this trip was likely to turn into a moot point. Though time wasn't on my side, I decided to give it a try. The focus was on rock piles and other more permanent structure. This didn't yield any results.

So I went back to my bread and butter: deadsticking at the Flats. It produced a few more fish, including another one in the 11-inch range. I ended my day with a total of 35 fish, including 26 smallmouth bass. My top five fish totaled 51.25 inches. I was in 10th place as the sun set.

But that didn't mean the action was over. Far from it. There were folks fishing in my region in different time zones, meaning they still had daylight to work with. Knowing that after-dark bites are hard to come by, even in the warmest of months, I decided to chill in the proverbial clubhouse and watch how things played out. In fact, Lyza and I went and visited our friends Shawn and Cassie at their home in nearby Mt. Calvary. Enjoying a few whiskey-cokes, I kept an eye on the standings as we chatted and played cribbage.

Sure enough, one of my competitors, a gentleman named Rickie Cole, was on the charge. As the gap began to close, I realized finishing in the top 10 meant more to me than I realized, even if I was only in a field of 30. I became addicted to the app. I found myself refreshing it every few minutes, feverishly hoping for an update. I definitely wasn't being a good friend at this point because I was so focused on my phone, but I couldn't help myself. There were still two hours left at this juncture and the gap between Rickie and I continued to dissipate.

When time was up, I closed my eyes, giving in to the

anticipation and nervousness, and refreshed the app once more. By the slimmest of margins—a quarter of an inch to be exact, I had clung to my top-10 standing. I finished in the top third of my first-ever bass fishing tournament, without a boat, on a day filled with crappy weather.

I was incredibly proud of myself for having managed a finish like this while fishing exclusively from shore with less than a week to fully prepare. Exhaustion was also beginning to get the better of me. I fished from sunup to sundown, adrenaline pumping, mind racing. It felt like I was stuck in the "on" position for the better part of the last 16 hours. The addiction of tournament fishing began to take hold.

CHAPTER 12

Bass Tournament No. 2: The Best Fishing Weekend of My Life

Fish Nos. 239-455

As the end of September rolled around, so came my second bass tournament. Originally intended to be my first dive into the competitive bass fishing world, this was a weekend-long event. Other than spanning three days, it was structured exactly like the tournament I fished earlier in the month. The country was divided into regions. Any public waters in your region were fair game and the five longest bass counted toward your score. Everything was submitted via the tournament app.

Unlike the previous "members only" event I participated in, this tournament, open to the public, was considerably larger. There were 185 anglers competing in my region, compared to the mere 30 from a few weeks prior. I would have to bring my

A-game to finish like the one I had spent the past two weeks bragging about.

The fall bite was in full swing. As water temperatures begin to drop from their summer peaks, bass begin to get more active while anticipating the arrival of winter. This made me relatively optimistic about my chances.

With a day off from work on Friday, I was confident I could get my weekend off to a strong start. My plan was to get five solid fish on the board during the first day, then turn my attention to targeting larger fish, but perhaps fewer, on Saturday and Sunday.

Again, the Sheboygan River ultimately played a crucial role in my success.

Just after sunup, about a quarter to 7, I made my way to the Old Plank Road Trail. The paved trail runs roughly 21 miles from the outskirts of Sheboygan westward to the county line. One of the parking lots along the way is just outside of Sheboygan Falls.

My family and I used to ride bikes here when I was younger. Once in a while, my dad and I would end our bike trips with a quick fishing session by the river bend near the parking lot. We would catch smallmouth and rock bass on rooster tail spinners.

This spot had proven difficult to solve earlier in the season, but I knew it held fish. When it was good, it could be very good. A couple of nights before the tournament, I managed to catch 22 smallmouth bass in under an hour. It seemed like I might have finally figured this spot out.

Nightcrawlers were the flavor of the day, presented on bottom rigs. I had a pair of lines in the water. It was a gorgeous 70 degrees, with the sun making its presence known early.

The first bites came quickly, which I had learned in my limited experience, is a sigh of relief in a tournament setting even if you have roughly 72 hours to find five big bass. My second fish of the day was a little over 13 inches, more than a half-inch longer than my largest of the first tournament. This was a good start.

I pulled nearly two dozen smallmouth during the 90 minutes or so I spent in this location before I decided to move on in search of faster-paced action.

My previous experiences at the Flats had me feeling good about my chances as I pulled up shortly after 9 a.m. It turned out that feeling was warranted, as I caught several fish that increased my total length. Each of my top-five bass were now at least 10 inches long. This was how I hoped to get out of the gates.

Eventually, I made my way to the dam, only to discover that some adjustments had been made to the gate that altered the rate water was allowed to flow in the river below. This effectively eliminated one of the slower pockets of water I generally target when I'm here which, under normal conditions, is one of my best spots to fish from shore in this area.

I decided to stay with my plan and put in some time here, but the shifting flow of the water slowed the fishing a good deal. Generally speaking, most of the hungry bass I've found in this portion of the Sheboygan spend time in the seams of water between the current and the more stagnant water. This gives the fish the best of both worlds. It keeps them close enough to the current that often provides oxygen-rich water and fresh food that gets swept up from the bottom, but without having to exert the vast energy needed to hold steady in the middle of that current.

But today, with the gate at the top of the dam opened, the river appeared to be one giant stream of steady current.

After flipping in a few small fish, I decided to take a lunch break. My tally for the day stood at 67 fish, mostly smallmouth, though a few straggler rock bass and even a couple of bluegill made their way onto my hooks.

After going back home and taking time for nourishment and recharging between noon and 2 p.m., I poked around at River Park. My pre-fishing gave me reason to believe the old lagoon still had some life in it. While this spot didn't typically produce large bass, this would be the time of year any impressive specimens would be likely to show themselves. I found only a few hungry bluegills and not much else.

A little after 3 p.m., I moved back to the dam to see if the fish, given more time to adjust to their new surroundings, had become a bit more active. That proved to be a lost cause. With sunlight fading away, I returned to the bike trail, where I had started my day.

When I arrived around 6:30 p.m., I was greeted by a host of eager fish. The action was steady, forcing me to downsize to a one-rod setup. The strikes came so quickly that I even resorted to holding my rod rather than placing it in the rod holder because, more often than not, the rod tip would be bouncing away before I even managed to get the rod out of my hands. At one point, I caught a bass on 10 straight casts.

As the day came to a close, I had 114 fish, nearly half my fish total for the entire season. The total length of my five longest fish was 60 inches on the head, over nine inches above where I finished my first tournament. I was satisfied but knew I needed bigger fish in the hours to come. I sat in 27th place, though many of my fellow competitors, probably stuck at work, hadn't ventured out yet.

The results thus far showed that I certainly knew where the active fish were, but now the game was catching larger ones. Switching tactics seemed like the right call on Day 2, although that may sound crazy given my fish total from the day before.

My day began with a trip out to Terry's for a few dozen large fathead minnows. Though my desired size of fatheads is labeled as "large," these fish top out at about 2-3 inches. Fall bass are keen on feeding on minnows and I wanted to play into that by offering them a bait closely resembling what they were likely already feeding on.

With a cooler full of lively little fish in tow, I headed off to the spot that produced most of my scoring fish on Day 1: the Flats.

I opened the morning with a three-rod setup. Two had single hooks tipped with minnows, the other with a nightcrawler. I believed in my new strategy, but didn't want to completely sell out until I had proof of what was actually working.

As the sun rose and the temperatures warmed, the rod tips began moving. The nightcrawler rod was the top producer in the early going, but the fish offered up by the river were undersized.

Then one of the minnow rods went for the first time. The bait was absolutely hammered as the rod tip curled into a pleasing C-shape and stayed that way. I gave the line a tug and the weight on the other end felt significant. Against my better judgment, I opted to flip the fish over the chain-link fence and onto shore. This one was solid. At 12 inches even, it was a nice improvement over my previous catches and would pad my score lightly. Maybe I was on to something with these minnows.

The more time passed, the more the fish began to prefer the minnows. I landed a 12.5-incher that bumped up my score. My smallest scoring fish was now at one foot even. My largest remained the second fish I caught on Friday morning. But I had a hunch I was currently in the spot that would change that.

A short time later, another dramatic strike. When I set the hook, nothing happened. The weight just clung to the bottom, stubborn as a mule. This fish was a game-changer; of that I was certain.

As bad luck would have it, the fish hit the line on the far right of my three-rod setup. If I was to walk this fish to shore, I would have to navigate the other two lines along the way.

The fish darted toward the current. Sure enough, this one was solid. I needed this one. As it moved to the middle of the river, I used the added spacing to my advantage, lifting my line above the other two rods and maneuvering around them. I resumed the fight once I was free and clear on the other side.

My adversary began using the current to its advantage—or so it thought. In reality, the fish was simply making a beeline toward my desired landing spot. I walked with the fish downstream until I was at the water's edge. The gap between me and the end of my line was quickly closing.

I reeled up one more time and hunched over to secure the fish, or at least that's what I thought I was doing. The bass gave a determined shake of its head and, all of a sudden, the pressure was gone. The fish had escaped. This one stung. I lost my largest fish of the weekend just feet from shore.

Needing time to reset mentally, I continued to fish the spot. It produced a few more fish, but they all paled in comparison to the one that got away. Isn't that always how it works?

By mid-morning, a change of scenery seemed in order. If nothing else, it would help me get back into a better headspace. So I went back to the dam, armed with new bait and a slightly different approach. I hoped to reverse the misfortunes I endured here the day before.

Things went according to plan. The fish were much more active and willing to aggressively attack the minnows I was offering. The catches lacked size, but there were more of them than I experienced the day before. To me, that was a sign I was on the right track.

When I broke for lunch, I had 37 fish to my credit for the day and I had increased the total length of my top five fish by more than two inches.

Feeling revitalized, I was off to Plymouth to give the Mullet River a go. This spot had let me down during my last tournament, but I felt warmer weather would bring the location back to more favorable conditions that would force the fish present to show some signs of life.

Logically, I started fishing in the last spot I had caught a smallmouth. Two rods out, one with a minnow and another with a nightcrawler. Radio silence. This wasn't good.

I advanced toward the dam. Though it is significantly smaller than the one in Sheboygan Falls, it's an imposing figure when you're standing directly next to it. I stood on a small patch of concrete that was exposed by the lower water levels. The river is all of a few yards wide at this juncture. An apartment building butts right up to the far bank. I've often wondered what it would be like to live in one of those units and get to wake up to a view of the river each morning.

There was a small patch of rapids, and just beneath them was a relatively calm pool of deeper water. I dropped a line in with a minnow attached and almost instantly had a bite. It was a tiny smallmouth, but it was something, and more than this spot had given me in recent weeks.

The pool was roughly 10 square feet. But I had a hunch there were more fish hiding. I went back in with a fresh minnow and, sure enough, got another bite. This one felt like it had some shoulders to it. I pulled the fish ashore and my suspicions were confirmed. It was solid, but not overly large. I put it to the measuring board and it came out at 12 inches even. Not enough to increase my total. But I could feel the momentum beginning to shift and I became re-energized.

I pulled 8 fish out of that little pool, but none of them were bigger than that 12-incher. I moved up above the dam into the Millpond. Things got quiet again. Just as I was picking up my last rod, a small northern pike appeared in hot pursuit of my minnow. It accelerated and latched on. After a brief skirmish, he was on land. A nice little bonus fish released to grow and be caught another day.

My day concluded back in Sheboygan Falls as I returned to River Park where I fished Friday afternoon. This time, however, I was fishing the river between the two bridges that connected the park to the downtown portion of the city.

I was all-in on minnows at this juncture. A few bass were cooperative, but none of the stature the situation required to improve my standing. I caught two more pike, including a 22-incher. Unfortunately, I wasn't in the northern business this weekend.

Day turned to night and I returned home. But that was when my tournament fishing addiction got the better of me. I spent a chunk of the evening browsing the internet for nighttime bass fishing tips. I wanted to squeeze every ounce I could out of my remaining weekend. Sparked by my homework, I decided to head to the Flats for the first time that day—at 9 p.m.

Somehow, I had convinced myself that I had a fighting chance. I tossed a couple of minnows out and hoped for the best. It was slow and the buzz I achieved through my new knowledge was beginning to wear off.

That's when I caught a rod tip moving out of the corner of my eye. I excitedly ran over to the rod and, grabbing it, ripped upward. There was a fish on. I pulled it over the railing. It was a bullhead. Not a shock, given the time of night, but somewhat surprising in late September. The whiskered critter proved to be the only fish I would catch that night.

Day 2 concluded with another 57 fish on the books and 171 for the weekend. Even though I increased my scoring total to 62.25 inches, I fell to 60th place in the standings. Only one day of fishing remained.

Dawn broke on the final day of the tournament. And, as I had the day before, I found myself beginning my day in the truck en route to Terry's for a fresh stock of fatheads.

My plan was to fish my hottest spots and any remaining locations I hadn't hit yet that I couldn't live without.

I returned to the Flats, this weekend's honey hole. The fish appeared to be a little more sluggish than they were in the days before (the nearly 100 fish I pulled out of these waters in the previous 48 hours probably played a role in this), but they were definitely still feeding. I caught a good smallie, a shade under 13 inches and a nice little bump to my score.

Again, I was going with a three-rod approach. I pulled out all the stops on the tournament's final day.

While finicking with a tangled line, I noticed that one of my rods had climbed the fence and was caught up in one of the links. The rod tip was feverishly pounding up and down, a sure indication there was a fish on the line and it was a large one.

I sprinted over to my rod and set the hook. I felt plenty of pressure. Could this be the time for redemption?

The fish rose to the surface and sailed upriver. It was indeed big, the biggest of the weekend so far. I couldn't let history repeat itself. I carefully managed the drag, walking the tightrope of keeping enough tension to keep the fish hooked, but not applying so much force that the fish could escape or the line would fail.

I made my way down to the rock I was standing on when I

lost the big one a day prior. I kept the line tight, slid the fish toward shore and placed my thumb into its mouth. I clamped down and brought the fish out of the water. This one was going to count and it was a beauty.

With a gorgeous dark green hue and detailed black accents, the fish measured 17 inches long. At the time, it was the second-largest smallmouth of my life. And I caught it during a tournament! I was pumped. No matter what happened the rest of the day, I could be confident that I put my best foot forward throughout the weekend. There weren't many fish of this caliber in the system and I landed one of them when it really mattered.

The day continued and I steadily progressed from spot to spot. More fish gave in to the temptations of my tasty offerings, but they were all too small to make an impact on the leaderboard.

Rain was beginning to fall, spurring memories of the one-day tournament I fished a few weeks earlier. But if that experience taught me anything, it was that there were still fish to be had when the weather took a turn. So I kept at it.

Per my dad's suggestion, I fished a new spot on a walking trail on the east side of the river. I hooked into another solid bronze back, but it slipped the hook a few yards from shore. More heartbreak. While I was out of contention for a high finish, that fish surely would have helped my prospects.

I moved to my in-laws, where the fish could be plentiful but often small. I hadn't fished the spot in a few weeks and wasn't quite sure what to expect.

I used a single rod, the line tipped with a fathead, and a sinker would keep the bait submerged. I caught a couple smallies, but the sinker quickly became an issue, catching on the rocky bottom. These snags cost me precious time.

Out of necessity, I took the sinker off and used the combined weight of the hook and minnow to get the job done. The payoff was instant. Hyperactive fish came out from their rocky hiding places and snapped at the minnow before I even began reeling. I caught a dozen smallmouth, but my scoring stalled and time was running out.

A Hail Mary remained in my pocket, though it required substantial effort. With the rain slowing, I decided it was now or never. I put on my waders and went back to the dam.

Though I had spent extensive time fishing this stretch over the course of the weekend, I hadn't worked this particular part. On the far shore, across from the park, a pool of deep water sits between the dam's base and a small island. While I hadn't been in this spot recently, my childhood experiences taught me this location often held larger bass of the kind I so desperately needed.

I sloshed my way across the shallow river bed. I packed lightly for this short journey. Dry spots were at a premium and I would have to carry most of my possessions for the duration of my outing. My pack included my backpack, one rod, some spare hooks and sinkers, the minnow cooler and my measuring device.

Once I found a suitable perch near the side of the dam, a couple of 10-inchers jumped on shore, but we were well past that now. I found a few more small ones, but my hopes were fading.

As a last attempt, I walked across the river to the deep pocket by the near side of the dam. I found a few more willing participants but they were also underachievers. So closed the book on my first three-day competitive bass fishing affair.

The final day of the tournament concluded with another 45 fish, bringing my weekend total to a cool 216 (all from shore). At the time, this accounted for almost two-thirds of my fish for the season. When the calendar expired at the end of December, the fish I landed this weekend made up nearly half of all the fish I caught during the year.

My top five fish totaled out at 67.5 inches, a 16-inch improvement from my first tournament. I took 73rd out of the 185 anglers in my region, many of whom were exclusively fishing from boats. This filled me with a sense of pride and the affirmation that maybe, just maybe, I could call myself an above-average angler.

Few things compare to the rush of competitive fishing. I learned a lot about myself over those three days: the importance of having a plan and knowing when or if to deviate from it, how positive self-talk is the key to maintaining a proper mindset, and how much fun can be had when you push yourself and follow your passion.

Sometimes, you have to put your money (in this case, $30) where your mouth is to discover what you are truly made of.

It was at this point that I started looking at the big picture and considering just how high my fish count could get.

CHAPTER 13

Fishing With My Brother-In-Law

Fish Nos. 467-471

My brother-in-law Mitchell is one of the smartest people I've ever met. He's a unique combination of book smarts matched with practicality and personality.

My sister Charlene met Mitchell at Port Washington High School after my sister transferred there for her junior and senior years. They started dating shortly after they graduated in 2011.

I will never forget the Thanksgiving when I walked out the front door of my parents' house to grab something from my truck when I stumbled upon Mitchell asking my dad's permission to marry my sister Charlene.

He had a bullet from a deer hunting rifle in one of his hands and joked with my dad that he was giving it to him in case my dad was upset about the proposition of Mitchell marrying into our family.

Mitchell is a man of many talents and diverse interests that range from computers and video games to photography. One of those interests is the outdoors. For whatever reason, I had only been hunting or fishing with him a handful of times up until this pandemic year of 2020. Looking back, it was a missed bonding opportunity. But I am grateful we have spent more time together outside and have taken better advantage of our shared hobbies.

It was mid-October and Mitchell, my dad and I had just concluded a duck hunting outing. The original plan was to go back out again in the afternoon, but our scouting had us feeling skeptical. Not wanting to be cooped up indoors, the three of us decided to go fishing.

We met at River Park, fishing rods in hand. I had two containers of nightcrawlers for the group. Deadsticking was the strategy as we took on the Sheboygan River (neither of these things should come as a surprise by now).

As we settled in, Mitchell noticed someone had left a dead carp by the base of a tree just yards from our spot. But, as he soon discovered, it wasn't dead. Though it was covered in sand and dry to the touch, the fish's gills were still moving. He handed me the fish and I gently held it in the water. This seemed like a lost cause, but it was worth a shot.

After a few minutes, the gill beats increased in pace. Signs of life! I slipped my grip down toward the tail and began gently rocking the fish back and forth in the current, trying to promote the flow of water through the gills. I could feel the carp's strength coming back ever so slightly, and I decided to release my grasp. The fish shook its tail twice and began to move toward the middle of the river, only to float back on its side. Too soon.

Mitchell went in after the fish that was just out of my reach.

He promptly slipped on the muddy bank and slid into the water, nearly up to his knees. So much for good karma. Though I give Mitchell a lot of credit, he never uttered a complaint about being damp on a cool fall afternoon.

The state of his pants and shoes didn't deter him. He secured the fish and returned it to me. We resumed the process once again. More time had passed and the fish seemed ready to make another go. This time, I only partially released my hand from its belly. Now it was kicking a little more aggressively.

Now I completely let the fish go and it began gingerly swimming downriver, still within sight of the bank. After a few tense moments, the carp eased its way into the depths of the river to swim another day. We had saved a little life. Mitchell's willingness to help, even after things took an unfortunate turn, says a lot about his character. His concern for the carp reflects the type of guy I have learned him to be.

With our good deed for the day completed, we got to fishing.

Looking back on it now, perhaps Mitchell did benefit from the bright side of karma. His rod was the first to go. A beautiful smallmouth bass leaped into the air and came down with a dramatic splash. This was a solid specimen.

He got the fish to shore and we took measurements. Fourteen inches—legal size for keeping in the state of Wisconsin. After posing for a picture, Mitchell placed the fish back in the water and the festivities commenced once again.

My dad managed a couple of smallies of similar stature, but that was it. We decided to move upriver to a spot across the bridge.

Mitchell set up his dead rod and began tossing with his baitcaster. I had mentioned to him earlier that I've caught many small northern pike in this stretch of the river. He said pike were one of his favorite fish to pursue. While his casts on this day didn't deliver any northerns, he was able to land another smallmouth on the dead rod.

At one point in the trip, my phone buzzed in my pocket. My brother-in-law Jake posted a link to a robotic swimming lure on my Facebook wall. I had never seen a lure quite like this before. I knew I needed to have it so I could explore what all of the fuss was about. So, while I was still on my phone, I went ahead and ordered one.

Meanwhile, my dad scored a few more plump bass and a pair of suckers. I got in on the action as well, with two smallies of my own. All in all, it was a fun, relaxing night of fishing. Before we went our separate ways, I asked Mitchell if he wanted to go again. He said he was interested. Two days later, we were back at it.

This time, armed with fresh knowledge of my kin, I decided to take Mitchell to the Glenbeulah Millpond. This offshoot of the Mullet River is a dynamite spot for pike through the ice in the winter months. A friend from high school introduced me to this location in college and my friends and I have spent many hours chasing tip-ups here in bitterly cold temperatures.

Glenbuelah Millpond holds lots of pike. Possibly too many, as evidenced by the small size of nearly all of the northerns I have caught here. Most of them are cookie-cutter specimens in the 12-to-14-inch range.

The water is generally pretty shallow, seldom reaching depths of more than five or six feet. The mucky bottom plays host to plenty of weed growth for the pike to hide in.

I recently began partaking in open-water fishing here and had found some success. This made me confident I could put Mitchell on some pike.

At my suggestion, he went with an orange and silver Little Cleo, a personal favorite of mine, especially in this spot. I chose to use fathead minnows and the new swimming lure I bought during our last outing at River Park.

By using both real minnows and the new robotic one, my goal was to simulate the experience we give the fish in wintertime in hopes of duplicating that level of success.

It was Mitchell who chose the better of the two options as he quickly had three pike to his credit.

Things slowed down after a while and Mitchell switched baits. At this point, I decided to do the same. He went with a floating Rapala and tied on the Little Cleo that produced the early success. This paid some dividends for us as we each scored one more northern.

As the sun began to slip under the horizon, an idea struck. I tossed Mitchell my phone and asked him to shoot a quick video. I gave an unrehearsed, brief rundown of must-have pike fishing tools. Whether I realize it or not, part of me is always looking for ways to make content that allows me to share my passion for the outdoors, even when I don't have a particular plan for amplifying it.

This inherent passion for sharing is part of what drove me into journalism early in my career. I find a lot of enjoyment and fulfillment through learning new things and being able to share that knowledge with others.

When I got home later that night, I edited the video, uploaded it to YouTube, and shared it on Instagram. "We need to make more of these," I thought to myself as I finished up.

This got me thinking about a conversation I had with Mitchell earlier in the night before we parted ways at the Millpond.

"If you ever want to do this again, we can use my camera equipment," he told me. "I have a microphone that would give us much better sound quality."

Deciding to take him up on his offer, I fired off a text message. The next day, we were at it again.

Back at River Park, the plan was to shoot a product review of my new swimming lure. But the fishing action got in the way.

Shortly after our arrival, one of my dead rods, tipped with a minnow, started going crazy. I ran over to it and set the hook. This fish was a particularly feisty one. As I inched the fish toward shore, I could tell the hook was coming loose. "Mitchell, get the net," I said frantically.

He quickly came down to the water's edge and scooped the fish. It was a chunky 16.5-inch smallmouth, the third largest of my life.

Not knowing what else to do, I set the fish in the minnow cooler so it could catch its breath and instructed Mitchell to grab his camera. I had a video idea.

We shot a quick video about how to properly handle a bass, a topic I have learned a lot about over the course of many years. Because I view myself primarily as a catch-and-release fisherman, this topic was close to my heart.

We cranked out the video and released the fish.

By the time the night ended, we had each caught a pair of smallmouth. Together we had shot one complete video and had most of the footage for the one we initially intended to film.

I was hardly home for an hour when I got a message from Mitchell. The raw files were in a shared drive and he was hard at work editing the video. When I woke up in the morning, I had a link to the edited version that included b-roll and stock music, ready for posting.

It was at that point "Nathan Woelfel Outdoors" was born. The concept wasn't fully-baked (it still isn't) but I knew I had to run with it while the spirit was moving me. With the pandemic raging, my side hustle as a freelance sports writer was on hold.

I hadn't been doing much writing and I wanted something to fill that gap in my life.

Somewhere over the course of this fishing season, I found my voice. I realized that, with a little bit of thought and effort, I could help others enjoy the outdoors in their own way. This just happened to be the moment when the proverbial lightbulb went off.

With momentum on our side, things quickly escalated. Just a few weeks later, we shot another video. Without being asked, Mitchell created a logo that he added to the front end of my latest video. I took that logo and got some mock-ups created of it on the front of a variety of baseball caps. Before long, everyone in my family was proudly sporting Nathan Woelfel Outdoors hats.

In the meantime, I built a website, and this book project was born.

These days, I am writing articles for nathanwoelfeloutdoors.com on a weekly basis as well as producing a corresponding podcast two times a month. I am sharing my knowledge and experiences in the outdoors to help inspire others to go out and discover the wonders of the natural world. This endeavor has provided me with a continual source of fulfillment as I hope to teach others about my passions of fishing, hunting, birding, and cooking.

It's amazing what can come from a few fish and spending quality time with family. I wouldn't be doing any of this if not for my brother-in-law.

CHAPTER 14

Finally Cashing in on the Salmon Run

Fish Nos. 480-481

This probably won't come as much of a surprise but, whenever I find myself outside, I'm frequently thinking about fishing. Any time I see a body of water, my brain whispers "Hmm, I wonder if I could fish that?" When the answer is yes, I then ask myself, "Well, how would I go about fishing that water?"

The events leading up to catching a pair of king salmon during the fall run are a perfect example of how quickly my brain can switch over to fishing mode.

It was a crisp afternoon in late October when my wife and I were out for a walk at a local nature preserve. The property is a mix of upland tall grasses and woodlands divided by the Pigeon River, a tributary to Lake Michigan.

The original intent of our trip was to get some exercise and enjoy a brief birding expedition. But it eventually ended up being a scouting mission for angling adventures that were to happen sooner rather than later.

We slowly strolled along the path adjacent to the river and I caught myself taking a glimpse toward the river bottom, looking for signs of life. The gravel river base and shallow water presented ideal conditions for observing fish.

Just as we were about to turn around and head back to the truck, the sound of splashing water drew our attention. We unknowingly had spooked a large king salmon out from its resting spot along the bank and it was now darting upriver. My wife was shocked by its size. I was more shocked by its sheer presence, especially considering how late in the season it was and how far away from the lake we were.

Generally speaking, the king salmon run in our neck of the woods begins in early September and concludes by mid to late October. When the salmon mature sexually, between the ages of two and four years old, they leave the comforts of Lake Michigan and head into its tributaries to spawn and complete their life cycles.

The onset of the journey is sparked by biology. The fish are able to sense when it is time to go. Water temperatures and flow indicate when it is time for their final odyssey to begin.

Tens of thousands of fish make this trek each autumn, sometimes venturing 15 to 20 miles from the lake, being stopped only by dams on the river—or death.

I was excited by the fact there were still a few salmon hanging around in the river and my mind immediately fixated on pursuing them. From then on, our journey to the parking lot became a fish-finding effort and, sure enough, there were a few more straggler kings hanging out in this narrow section of the Pigeon.

My blood was pumping as we left. I knew I had to get back soon. The clock was ticking.

The morning after our walk, I was able to clear some time in my schedule for a trek back to the river bottom. I took the back entrance to the property and walked a road through a neighboring park, hoping to shorten the distance from my parking spot to where I last saw the salmon. I thoroughly scoped the downriver stretch of water for the potential existence of more fish, but all I found was two more fishermen, mere yards from my target.

I was a little surprised by this discovery. It was just before noon on a Monday, after all. I thought the middle of the workday was the ideal time to avoid additional fishing pressure. Apparently, these two gentlemen felt the same way.

But, at this point, I was committed. With my spinning rod in hand, I slowly crept ahead and worked my way to the river. From there, I gently proceeded up the shoreline, probably 50 yards upriver from where I saw the first king the day prior.

Initially, there was no action. I continued to methodically work up the bank with my eyes constantly scanning the water that was only yards from me. Lo and behold, there she was. Despite her large stature, this female king salmon would have been easy to miss. In fact, my money says the other fishermen I encountered probably walked right past her. Her appearance was reduced to little more than a shadow with just the slightest bit of her dorsal fin protruding from the current. This subtle, unnatural disturbance in the water gave up her position. She was less than 10 yards from me, seemingly hovering in the relatively clear water.

I tipped my single hook with a spawn sack and went to work. I didn't want to harass the fish, but it seemed silly to pass up on what appeared to be a high-percentage opportunity for success.

Now, I'll be the first to admit a spawn sack probably wasn't the ideal bait for this scenario. There comes a point in the run where salmon simply stop eating or, at the very least, they eat significantly less. Any bites you get are purely reactionary, sparked by a burst of anger or defensiveness. A spinner or crankbait—heck, even a live minnow—would have been a better call here. But in my excitement, I failed to make a thorough plan and showed up with what I had on hand.

I started by placing the bait a couple of feet in front of her. The single quarter-ounce sinker kept the bait in place in the current as the spawn sack held at her eye level. I repeated this several times, but she didn't move an inch.

At that point, I knew I had to get a reaction bite out of her. So I became more aggressive, plopping the spawn sack right in front of her. We're talking a matter of inches. I would slowly pull it across the bottom and drag it near her nose, figuring it was my best chance to annoy her.

As time wore on, I got gutsier. I plopped the bait closer and closer until—whoops, too close. She shot out of the middle of the river and to the far bank. I spooked her, plain and simple. The good news was I could see her new location and it wasn't far from where I was standing. In a calculated manner, I worked my way up to her new hideout. Once there, I employed the same tactic I used previously.

After a few casts, the moment I had been waiting for finally came. As I slowly inched the spawn sack across the bottom, her big jaw snapped. Instant tension overwhelmed the end of my line and the fight was on.

She ran back downriver, crossing over my position in the process. She was clearly looking for deeper water so she could garner more leverage on the hook, or maybe some kind of branch or rock to wrap the line around so she could make her escape.

Trying my best not to apply excessive force, I eventually got the upper hand and guided her back to the shallows. From there, I was able to slowly walk her back to the shoreline and beach her on the bank. (I didn't have a net on me. In hindsight, that was really stupid. But more on that later.)

There she was. The fight was over. I took some pictures and sent a text to my dad and another to my wife. All told, the fish measured 37 inches and scaled out at a hair over 21 pounds—the second-largest king of my life.

I made the decision to keep her. And while I completely understand why that is frowned upon in many

regions of the country, let me explain why it's a little different in Wisconsin before you decide to get mad at me and stop reading.

Most of the king salmon in our portion of Lake Michigan are stocked by the Department of Natural Resources. This is because of the general lack of natural reproduction, particularly in this area. Due to a variety of environmental factors, not many four-year-old kings that make their life-ending runs up the tributaries produce viable offspring. Of the few that actually hatch, an even smaller percentage live long enough to find their way back to the big water. This is partially because of the drastic water temperature swings that can occur with the frequently-changing depths of the tributaries in this part of the state.

With that in mind, and since this salmon was knocking on death's door anyway, I made the call to keep her. I was able to salvage some of the meat (fish at this stage of their lives are literally rotting from the inside out) and was able to secure enough eggs to have a plethora of spawn sacks for next season.

In hindsight, I could have let that fish go. In the future, I probably will. But this was my first-ever salmon from the run and I was excited. So I opted to bring her home, though I felt the need to reassure myself that this was OK. After all, I was legally allowed to keep her but I was uneasy about doing so because, as these fish make their end-of-life journeys, their meat begins to turn soft and dark rather than the welcoming pink color it possesses during the rest of their lives.

Meat from a mature, spawning salmon simply doesn't taste as good. But I figured that, if nothing else, she would provide me with more than enough eggs to make the spawn sacks required for the following year.

I must concede, I spent the next few days feeling a bit torn about my decision, especially as I read more and more about how viable salmon are treated in other portions of the country. That includes some parts of neighboring Michigan that have a relatively higher rate of natural reproduction and where many fish caught during the run are leased so they can complete the spawning process. That's when I decided that any river salmon for the remainder of the year were going right back where they came from.

A few weeks later, my wife and I were on another Sunday afternoon walk in the nature preserve. At this point, it was early November. And while I was pretty convinced there weren't any kings left in the river, I couldn't keep myself from continuing to scout.

Sure enough, we stumbled upon three more fish and at least two of them were kings. One of them was turning white. We observed them for a while as they slowly drifted in and out of the current on their way upstream.

I knew what I would be doing on lunch break the next day. This time, I came bearing a cooler full of minnows to compliment my spawn sacks. I figured the darting of a live fish was far more likely to annoy a spawning king than a sack full of stagnant eggs.

The scouting mission began about 50 yards upriver from where we saw the fish the previous day. My first surveillance scan yielded nothing, but a second run-through produced something suspicious. At first glance, it appeared to be some brush caught on a stick. But a closer examination revealed it to be the beat-up dorsal fin of a male king salmon (its kype gave away its gender, as did the "milk" running down its side).

A kype is a hook-like formation on a fish's jaw that appears on some male salmon during the run. The aforementioned "milk" is a slang term for sperm. The presence of these two indicators made it certain that the specimen was indeed a male.

Having been eager to locate the fish, I placed myself a bit too close for comfort. He sat about five yards from me in roughly three feet of water. I slowly backed up and rigged my line. I lip-hooked a large fathead minnow on a single hook and went at it.

The plan was to slowly and repetitively swim the minnow across the fish's face until it got pissed. It was a crude plan, but I felt it was my best bet. As I learned later, this is not at all how an angler should approach this situation.

It only took a handful of casts for the salmon to snap. Hooked up, baby! The drag began singing and the battle was on. This guy decided that sprinting upriver was his best shot, so he took off like a dart into the shallows leaving a noisy wake as went.

In my head, I already had this fish counted on my personal scoreboard. That proved to be a mistake.

I worked him into a sandbar in the middle of the river. He was beached and I was about ready to call this fight. But as I approached to pick him up, the fish freaked. And with one big headshake, he was off the hook both literally and figuratively.

He didn't go far—just a few yards from his original position. I took a moment to catch my breath and collect myself. I applied a fresh minnow to my hook and cautiously approached.

While the fish seemed to be a little more leery this time around, he proved to be equally annoyed. After a few more casts, he lunged forward at my minnow and took a big swipe, gulping my minnow. Round 2 was officially here, only minutes after the disappointing conclusion of the first.

I was more level-headed about this encounter. No more counting chickens before they're hatched.

This time, the fish opted to dive into a deep pocket of water to my right. He hit the pool with aggression and zoomed toward a downed log that was partially sticking out of the water. As it turns out, that was his ticket to freedom. He wrapped my line in a submerged branch and slipped the hook, disappearing into the depths for the remainder of my session.

I headed home, tail between my legs. I had somehow managed to lose the same fish twice in a matter of minutes. Talk about a bruised ego.

That experience didn't sit well with me so, the next day, I decided to try again. This time I had a landing net with me. Though it was smaller than the ideal size, it was all I had and definitely better than nothing.

I went back to the location of the previous day's disappointments and there was no sign of the king. I continued my walk downriver and was pleased to discover that one of the kings we had seen in that spot during our Sunday walk was still there. So I unpacked and started in.

This fish was wise and seemed quite vivacious given how late in the season it was. It sensed my presence along the bank and quickly skirted to the middle, where the water was deeper. I lost sight of the fish, but decided to pursue it in the water.

I walked down the bank and entered the water at a shallow point downriver. I then walked the far bank back up to where I last saw the fish. No luck.

After trudging back to my starting point, I again caught sight of the fish. I flipped a minnow in its direction and it bolted.

This seemed like a lost cause. I gave the fish about 15 minutes to show itself, once it didn't I decided to throw in the towel. I took a slow walk back to my truck, but I kept scanning the river as I went.

I made it a few hundred yards upriver when I spotted a familiar sight—a dorsal fin that sure looked a lot like brush hung up on a stick. It was the fish from yesterday. Game on, once again.

He was nestled up near the far shore with plenty of room in front of him. My plan was to cast upriver from him and let the current drift my bait right into his face.

After a couple minutes of this, he finally had enough. His wide jaw flared and he chomped down on a mouth full of hook. Despite being in the waning hours of his life, the fish seemed to have plenty of energy for a fight.

He advanced upriver to my left as I tried to maneuver my rod around trees while trying to formulate a plan for how I was going to land this thing. The fish eventually tired out and drifted slowly near the shore I was standing on.

Eventually, I was able to get him downriver to where my net was. Frantically leaning over the steep embankment, about four feet above water level, I tried to strategically place my net just behind his tail with the hope the current would float him right into it.

The fish turned around and bolted head-first into the net. "Oh, awesome," I thought to myself.

Not awesome, as it turned out. As I went to lift the net with my right hand, the back half of the fish slid out of the net and back into the river. The fight was back on.

After a few more minutes, I was able to weather the storm and get the fish back to shore. I laid down on my stomach rod in one hand, net in the other. This time, my plan worked. The fish drifted into the net tail-first and I brought him ashore. The "one that got away" had only done so for about 24 hours.

I took a few pictures, a rough measurement of the length (a little more than 32 inches) and released the fish, ending our three-round tangle.

Overall, I was quite pleased that I was able to catch my first pair of lake-run salmon and, in a way, that is something I will always be proud of.

However, a few months later, I learned there were significant errors in my approach.

There are certain risks that come from trying new things and one of them is the potential of committing a faux pas or two when you're first starting out.

This can be unavoidable because, when partaking in new experiences, you don't know what you don't know. Sometimes, that means learning the hard way, as I did the following spring.

Wanting to learn more about fishing for lake-run trout and salmon, I booked a steelhead trip with a local guide. It was then, the March following my salmon adventures, that I discovered my thoughts on fishing the fall run were all wrong.

My guide told me that fishing for kings in fall or steelhead in spring is all about chasing the fish you can't see. While I was mostly correct about reactionary bites often being a key part of catching lake-run fish, he noted that I was much more likely to encounter fish that wanted to feed if I was targeting salmon that were in deeper river pools and not visible from shore.

He explained that the fish I was able to spot from shore a few months prior were likely just about to spawn or just concluding the process and that, in his eyes (and the eyes of many other anglers), pursuing those fish wasn't considered sporting.

Though nothing would ultimately come of it, these fish had one thing in mind: reproduction.

"You wouldn't want someone walking in on you and your special lady in the bedroom, would you?" My guide asked.

That example really drove the point home. I felt like an idiot.

At the time, I played it off with some sort of stupid joke along the lines of, "You're right, these fish will soon be on their death beds, the least I can do is let them get laid."

But my guide's lighthearted observation really got me thinking.

I pride myself on being a thoughtful and ethical angler and, the more my guide and I spoke about the situation, the more I realized that I probably had fallen short in that endeavor during my outings on the Pigeon River the previous fall.

Though I may have a case to plead ignorance, it did little to ease the guilt I felt. From that moment forward, I promised myself that I would take the information I had gained from my guide and use it to grow into a more well-informed and respectful fisherman.

CHAPTER 15

Calling an Audible for No. 500

Fish Nos. 482-501

The spring-like stretch of weather we enjoyed in early November of 2020 in Wisconsin was projected to come to an abrupt end, thanks to an approaching cold front.

Though not always driven by the calendar, there comes a time each year when winter formally announces its arrival. When this transition happens, there's no going back to the mild feeling of fall.

Winter brings with it a special brand of cold. It can be felt during the days when the chill of the morning air lingers a little longer than it used to and the frosty breezes begin to grip your skin. It's almost as though the entirety of the natural world slows down.

We were about to enter this time period in eastern Wisconsin and I knew I had to get out bass fishing one more time before the smallmouth likely went into winter mode for the remainder of the year.

I took an early lunch break and drove over to Terry's, where

I acquired roughly 18 large fathead minnows. I got back in the truck fully intending to head to the Flats, a spot where I had enjoyed some decent success the evening prior. But as I headed back east, my mind began to wander.

As things stood, I had 481 fish for the year and I was growing concerned that I was running out of time to reach my goal of catching 500 fish this year. While I didn't begin the year with this milestone in mind, at some point along the way, I decided that 500 sounded like a nice round, impressive number.

Up until this point of the season, I had never gone on a fishing trip feeling that I had to catch a specific number of fish. But today was an exception. The number 19 kept bouncing around my head as I drove from Terry's to my spot on the bike trail, a spot that had been hit-or-miss throughout the season.

When the fishing was good, it was one of the best spots I had in my pocket. But when things were slow, an angler could be in for a long day.

Given how active the fish at the Flats seemed to be, I decided to take a gamble that bass would be even more active in a spot that was just as shallow and featured even slower-moving water. If there was a chance that I could haul in 19 fish on lunch break, this narrow stretch of the Sheboygan River that ran next to the bike path was the only place I could think of to make that happen.

I told myself I would give it 10 minutes to feel out the situation. I didn't even bother bringing my water bottle or my full tackle box down from my truck. I descended the stairs and got to work.

Quickly, the fatheads on bottom rigs began capturing the attention of the hungry smallmouth. However, the first few fish were easily able to skirt the hook.

After an early snag, I decided to switch one of the rods over to a weightless minnow setup. That proved to be the ticket. At first, the bites were nearly instant. Bronze flashes began appearing from the deeper pockets almost as soon as the minnow began its initial descent. In short order, I was up to six fish.

But it became apparent that I had a problem. Thanks to the vigor of each strike, my fish-to-minnow ratio was all out of whack. A few of the more aggressive smallies were able to rip the minnow off the hook by the tail, avoid the barb of the hook and swim away. The fish that did stick hit the bait so hard that it drove the minnow up the shank of the hook and onto the line. During the ensuing fight, the minnow would rip off the line and float downriver.

At this point, I still had my doubts that 19 fish in this short time frame was an attainable number. But it was beginning to seem like more of a possibility.

As I reached into my dwindling supply of fatheads, I scooped up the largest minnow in the bucket. It was easily double the size of the second-largest minnow in my possession—quite possibly triple. While it was highly unlikely that the smaller bass I had been catching were up to the task of inhaling this monster minnow, I reassured myself that any large bass hanging around would probably find this quite tempting.

I tossed a short cast downriver into the small pocket in front of me. As I began my series of short pops, the minnow came into view. Lo and behold, a sizable smallmouth appeared from behind a rock near the bank and began steamboating its way toward my bait.

I saw the flash, felt the tension, and set the hook. Connection! The fish screamed toward the middle of the current and took a hard left back downriver. With one more big head shake, it was gone.

It was a perfect microcosm of my day to this point. No trouble finding fish, plenty of trouble keeping them hooked.

After I was done feeling sorry for myself, I dinked and dunked my way to 13 fish before my minnow supply ran dry. Even as this hurdle presented itself, I already had my mind made up that I wasn't leaving this spot until I had my 500 fish for the year.

The way I saw it, I had three options: I could swallow my pride and head back to the bait shop for more minnows (though that would take precious time I didn't really have. (Remember, I was on lunch break.) I could run to the local gas station and scoop up some nightcrawlers and hope enough fish were in full-on summer mode that I could cross the finish line that way. Or, I could dig in my tackle box and try to find the right artificial bait.

No matter which path I chose, I was likely headed back to my truck. But before I made the trek up the hill to the parking lot, I rifled through my fishing backpack. And there it was: old reliable – a black and silver floating Rapala F7. The most classic of baits. Its subtle wiggle action combined with its ideal size meant the bait's appearance closely matched that of the minnows I was just using, making this option a no-brainer. The second I saw that lure, I knew it was my best chance to pull this off.

So I tied the Rapala on and got to it. I began by working the pocket that produced most of my fish. I used a simple, straight retrieve at a relatively slow pace as I worked against the current.

The first cast led to a fish. And let me tell you, after 45 minutes of losing fish left and right on a single hook, it was sure nice to be fishing with a pair of treble hooks.

Two casts later, I hooked up again. Four fish to go. I was going to reach my goal. I could feel it in my bones.

But then the action slowed down. Twenty or 30 casts passed without a strike. I began second-guessing my technique. I switched things up to start-and-stop retrieve. Give it a few cranks and quick pause. Three more cranks, quick pause. Maybe an added twitch here or there if the situation warranted.

The change of pace quickly yielded another fish, but things promptly slowed down again. My head was spinning at this point, second-guessing everything from my bait choice to my retrieve to my location. Could the well really run dry this close to the finish line?

I scored one more fish on the straight retrieve before I decided to head downriver a bit. I had not pulled a fish out of this portion of the river, but I had seen plenty of action there when I witnessed a handful of smallie feeding frenzies during the summer months.

After a few casts, a nice fish emerged from the depths and feigned a sluggish attempt at a bite in the general direction of my lure. It missed. I started to become concerned the fish were shutting off. Rain was imminent and the temperature was dropping slightly.

I slid farther downriver to a place I had moderate success at in the summer. I had a hunch the rocky shoreline structure was still holding fish.

As I began the retrieve on my first down-current toss, I almost immediately felt weight. Bingo! Another fish added to the tally and only one more to go.

Another toss to a similar position yielded a quick bronze flash and a missed connection. I began working the slower pockets to no avail. I then put the bait in a seam between the current and the slack water and there it was. Fish No. 500 made its way to shore. It was by no means a monster, but it was undoubtedly a trophy to me.

I snapped a quick picture and placed the fish back in the chilly water. Even though I needed to get back to my desk, I tossed out one final cast. And, sure enough, it came back with a fish on it.

Twenty smallmouth bass in the course of lunch break in mid-November. Definitely not the way I expected to cross my desired fish count threshold.

Ironically, one of the places I found the most difficult to solve throughout the season proved to be the key piece in me reaching my coveted milestone. This only added to the satisfaction.

A mix of emotions came with reaching my goal. I was certainly happy. How couldn't I be? I had put a lot of time and effort into this and 500 fish in less than 12 months is nothing to coff at.

In some way, I felt a sense of relief. Though I had not started the year with this particular goal in mind, as it came into focus, I became more passionate about reaching it. Reaching my goal was never the focal point of any of my fishing trips, but I still wanted to do everything in my power to make it happen. The fact that I did filled me with pride.

Finally, and most of all, I felt fortunate.

2020 was a tough year for so many people, myself included. The drastic changes in the way we, as a society, went through our daily lives were challenging. But I had fishing to help keep me sane.

Even amidst the struggles of the pandemic, I was able to enjoy time outdoors while learning new things, pushing myself, and reconnecting with an old passion.

Fishing regained its rightful place as one of the most joyous parts of my life.

Conclusion

2020 was the most special fishing season of my life. Not just because of the number of fish I caught, but because of the enjoyment I took from the process.

When I mentioned at the beginning of this book that I spend time fishing every single summer, I meant it. But this year took it to a new level. I rediscovered a piece of myself.

Never in my wildest dreams would I have envisioned what this season had in store for me—the big fish, the tournaments, the website, this book, any of it.

I ended the year with 502 fish in 133 trips, catching 17 different fish species across 12 bodies of water. Those totals are, in all likelihood, the highest of my life in any one season. My lack of record-keeping in previous years means that I will never know for sure, but I've made peace with that.

Just over 239 hours of my year were spent with a rod in hand. That equates to nearly 10 full days—time well spent, in my opinion.

Even though I didn't begin the season with a specific fish count in mind, I felt a sense of pride in breaking the 500-fish threshold.

Granted, numbers aren't everything when it comes to

enjoying fishing. As I was reminded throughout the course of these months, time in the outdoors is about relaxing, spending time with meaningful people, and connecting with the larger world around us.

But arriving at such a wonderfully round total brought me joy and gave me a reason to reflect on fishing's place in my life. Even in the midst of a once-in-a-lifetime pandemic, I was able to find peace, fulfillment, and happiness.

The conclusion of the 2020 fishing season brought with it a complex cocktail of feelings.

On the one hand, I felt a renewed energy in my attitude toward fishing. From now on, I plan to be much more intentional about making time for fishing and spending time in the outdoors in general. I know this will greatly increase the quality of my life in the years ahead.

On the other hand, I was sad the season was over. I was worried about the void I now had in my life and wasn't sure about how I would fill it during the winter months, particularly because of the disdain I felt for ice fishing at the time.

I ventured out on nine more open water trips after I caught fish No. 500, but only caught one more fish, a small northern pike at River Park just before the Sheboygan River froze up for the winter. During that time, it was clear that my fishing adventures were showing diminishing returns, but I tried my best to fight the inevitable conclusion of the open water season. I didn't want that part of my life to go away, even though its disappearance would only be temporary. But Father Time eventually won this struggle. You know what they say about all good things.

I'm incredibly grateful for the experiences I had throughout the year, both the good and bad. Through them, I learned a lot about fishing and a little about myself. I grew as an angler and a person.

In the seasons that followed, I went on to catch more than 1,500 additional fish. I even broke the 1,000-fish mark two seasons after my pandemic adventures. While several of those fish have their own memorable stories, I can honestly say that the 2020 fishing season provided more meaningful experiences than any other I can recall. There was just something about rediscovering my true love of angling and finding a dependable source of enjoyment during the most uncertain times.

As a goal-oriented person, I continue to look forward. The prospect of the future is exciting. There are so many places in this state that I want to fish in the coming years, and even more outside of Wisconsin that have my eye. This sport has a way of keeping an angler coming back for more. No matter how good the fishing has been, there always seem to be clearer waters with even more fish.

In future seasons, documenting my excursions is going to be even more of a priority than it was in the past. I can't believe I ever went on fishing and hunting trips and didn't write down my thoughts and experiences afterward.

Being the numbers guy I am, I also plan on starting each season with a specific goal for the number of fish I'd like to catch. I will be sure, however, to not let that data point get in the way of enjoying my time on the water to the fullest. I can't wait to see what the future holds.

I'm lucky to be able to share all of these adventures with you. Reliving these moments through the writing process puts a smile on my face. I hope you found these stories relatable, enjoyable, and maybe even helpful.

But most of all, I hope these stories inspired you to go create some of your own.

Thank you for going fishing with me. I'll see you on the water.

Made in the USA
Monee, IL
06 June 2023